SS ARMOR
On The Eastern Front
1943 - 1945

Velimir Vuksic

SS Armor
On The Eastern Front
1943 - 1945

Velimir Vuksic

Published by
J.J. Fedorowicz Publishing, Inc.
104 Browning Boulevard
Winnipeg, Manitoba
Canada R3K 0L7
Tel: (204) 837-6080
Fax: (204) 889-1960
e-mail: jjfpub@jjfpub.mb.ca
web: www.jjfpub.mb.ca

Printed in Canada
ISBN 0-921991-86-X

Printed by Friesens Printers, Altona , Manitoba, Canada

Titles by
J.J. Fedorowicz Publishing, Inc.

Publishers' Acknowledgements

We wish to thank you, the reader, for purchasing this book and all of you who have written us with kind words of praise and encouragement. It gives us the impetus to continue translating the best available German-language books and produce original titles. Our listing of books published is on the preceding page and can be viewed on our web site at *www.jjfpub.mb.ca*. We have also listed titles, which are near production and can be expected in the near future. Many of these are due to your helpful proposals.

We look forward to your continued comments and constructive criticism.

John Fedorowicz — Mike Olive — Bob Edwards — Ian Clunie

Editors' Remarks

When translating German military terminology, modern American Army terminology is generally used wherever an equivalent term is applicable. In cases where there may be nuances where we think the reader might enjoy learning the German term, we have included it parenthetically.

In cases where the German term is commonly understood or there is no good, direct English equivalent, we have tended to retain the German term, e.g., *Schwerpunkt* (point of main effort), *Auftragstaktik* (mission-type orders) etc. We have also retained German practice in unit designations, e.g., the *1./schwere Panzerjäger–Abteilung 654* means the First Company of the 654th Heavy Antitank Battalion. Arabic numerals indicate companies or company-sized units (e.g., batteries or troops) and Roman numerals represent battalions (or battalion-equivalents) within a brigade or regiment.

When referring to general staff officers, the German suffix of *i.G.* (*im Generalstab*) has been retained.

The reader should also be aware that the *Wehrmacht* used Central European Time when operating on the Eastern Front, sometimes resulting in apparent incongruencies (e.g., "daylight" attacks starting in the summer at 0200 hours).

In an attempt to highlight the specific German terminology, we have italicized German-language terms and expressions. Since most of the terms are repeated several times, we have not included a glossary. Since we assume the reader will already have a basic understanding of German rank terms and the terminology used for vehicles, we have likewise not included any separate annexes to the book to explain them.

Although much of the original German text makes use of extensive abbreviations, these have generally been written out in full in order not to confuse any reader who may not be familiar with German military abbreviations. This includes quotations from other sources and primary source material.

J.J. Fedorowicz Publishing, Inc.

Velimir Vuksic

About the Author

Velimir Vuksic, B.Sc., was born in 1954 in Zagreb, Croatia, where he completed his education and where he lives and works today. He graduated from the Faculty of Transport Sciences (University of Zagreb) in 1980. In 1978, he received his qualifications for aircraft engine engineering. Because of the war in Croatia, he was unable to complete his post-graduate studies at the Faculty of Mechanical Engineering. He performed aircraft maintenance at the local airport. For a time, he lived in Great Britain, where he visited numerous military museums. With the increased availability of personal computers, he began to work intensively in that field. He worked as a programmer until 1990, when he established his own publishing company, which is still in operation today. He has designed and published books, calendars and magazines. He has been creating illustrations for more than thirty years and is a permanent associate of Osprey Publishing and several military magazines, in which he writes columns on military technology and militaria.

In 1976, he purchased his first English-language book on German tanks and, over the years, has compiled a collection of over one thousand books and ten thousand photographs. In 1980, he fulfilled his mandatory military service in Belgrade, where he worked on tanks, artillery and other weapons. Since then, he has cooperated extensively with military museums throughout Europe. His previous hobbies included sport parachuting, horseback riding and diving. Today, his hobbies are war gaming, collecting tank models and military figurines, and occasional fishing trips. He is married and has a daughter.

Acknowledgement

The author and Publisher wish to express their deep gratitude to the staff of the **National Museum of Contemporary History** in Slovenia (Celoveska cesta 23, 1000 Ljubljana, Slovenia) for providing many of the photographs presented in this volume. We hope that this book justifies their trust.

Velimir Vuksic and J.J. Fedorowicz Publishing Inc.

Table of Contents

Foreword

Following its defeat in World War I, Germany was hit hard by economic and political crises. The government fell apart and, in the land under the influence of Russian bolshevism, a revolution took hold and led to the dethroning of the monarchy and the creation of a republic. In the elections for the National Assembly, the Social Democratic Party won and formed an interim government. Fearing a Communist revolution in Germany, the victors of the war permitted the interim government to arm 100,000 men and, in early 1919, the revolution was smothered. The economic crisis, uncertainty in the nation, unemployment and high inflation became the foundations for growing nationalism and extremism. Under these circumstances, Adolf Hitler began to build the National Socialist Party (*NSDAP*) from various right-wing and nationalist groups. Ernst Röhm, one of his original associates, began to create the *SA* units (*Sturm Abteilungen* − Storm Troops), a paramilitary organization of the *Nazi* party for the battle against the Communists and the left-wing forces.

In fact, the first fascist military organizations had their beginnings in such organized armed semi-military units, as the strike groups of the reactionary parties. Using scare tactics, terror and murder, they opened the path toward a dictatorship. With the support of the *SA* units, Hitler attempted to take power in Germany in 1923. His coup failed and he ended up in prison, his party was banned and the *SA* units disbanded. Following his release from prison in December 1924, Hitler renewed his party and again re-founded the *SA* units, though this time they were unarmed. The following year, he founded the protective units (*Schutzstaffeln*) from the 10 most trusted members of his party who would serve as his bodyguards during his political campaign through Germany. In the well-known Munich military memorial the *Feldherrnhalle*, Hitler officially proclaimed the *Schutzstaffeln*, SS for short, at a formal ceremony held on 9 November 1925.

However, as time passed, the *SA* units, with their extreme demands, began to hinder Hitler in his battle to take power and he formed new *SS* units, which marked the beginning of the struggle for power between the leaders of these two organizations. By the spring of 1926, 75 such units had been created. In January 1929, Heinrich Himmler was placed at the head of the *SS* units, which under his command grew to 450 officers and 25,000 men by the summer of 1932.

The great world economic crisis also struck Germany in 1930. In this country with high unemployment, Hitler announced his aggressive policies and re-armament. He saw high capital in this as the opportunity to strengthen his control (the leadership of the Army saw it as an opportunity to re-create Germany into a strong armed force) and to lead the people out of the economic crisis. In 1933, Hitler became Chancellor of the *Reich*. One year later, with the death of President Hindenburg, the functions of Chancellor and President were amalgamated and, with the appointment of Hitler to that position, all political power in Germany was formally transferred into the hands of the *Nazis*. With claims that he wanted to prevent anarchy from taking hold in Germany, Hitler's struggle for power ended on 30 June 1930, with a bloody putsch, in which 77 leaders of the *SA* were killed and the entire organization was politically marginalized.

Politically strengthened on 20 July 1934, Hitler proclaimed the 200,000 strong *SS* as a formation independent from the *NSDAP*. Hitler granted the *SS* formations special status. They were divided into units for internal use (*Allgemeine SS*), military *SS* units (*Waffen-SS*) and *SS* police units. The military *SS* units had within their composition combat units (*SS-Verfügungstruppe*) and special purpose units (*SS-Totenkopfverbände*).

On 19 March 1935, Hitler announced that he would reintroduce conscription and form the Army into 36 divisions. He also ordered that the *SS-Verfügungstruppe* be formed as a military force. The first to be formed was a group of *Stabswache* detachments, which were placed under the command of Josef "Sepp" Dietrich. The *Stabswache Berlin* was expanded and quickly converted to a motorized regiment of three battalions strong. It was named the *Leibstandarte SS Adolf Hitler (LSSAH)*. The next group formed was the *SS-Totenkopfverbände* at Dachau. Commanded by Theodor Eicke, it was responsible for the concentration camps. Three more regiments were formed; the *Deutschland*, *Germania* and *Der Führer*, each with 2,000 men. They were organized in the *SS-Verfügungsdivision*. Himmler selected Paul Hausser as its commander. By 1939, the *SS* men were trained as assault troops. In addition to the physical training, politics and ideology were an integral part of their training. Many of the *SS* units had an advantage over their Army counterparts because they were completely motorized and had the most modern arms and equipment. This gave the *SS* troops a high combat value.

Following the successful campaign in Poland in 1939, which saw the participation of the entire *SS-Verfügungstruppe*, with the exception of the *SS-Standarte 3 "Der Führer"*, Himmler formed two new divisions, the *SS-Totenkopf-Division* and the *SS Polizei-Division*. The growing number of *SS* formations concerned the Supreme Command of the Germany Army (*OKW*). On 2 March 1940, Himmler agreed to place the *SS* divisions under the control of the Army, thereby resolving this problem, and the title *Waffen-SS* became official.

In November 1940, *SS-Standarte "Germania"* was transferred from the *SS-Verfügungs-Division* and, together with the newly formed *SS-Infanterie-Regiment "Nordland"* and *SS-Infanterie-Regiment "Westland"*, and *SS-Artillerie-Regiment 5*, formed the new *SS-Division (mot) "Germania"*. *SS-Totenkopfregiment 11*, soon to be redesignated as *SS-Infanterie-Regiment 11*, replaced *SS-Standarte "Germania"* in the *SS-Verfügungs-Division* and, in December 1940, the division was redesignated as *SS-Division "Deutschland"*. In 1941, the division was further redesignated as *SS-Division "Reich"*. *SS-Division (mot) "Germania"* was redesignated as *SS-Division "Wiking"* in December 1940.

A total of 106 divisions participated in the *Blitzkrieg* across Holland, Belgium and France in May and June 1940. The *LSSAH* and the *SS-Verfügungs-Division* led the way, creating a fighting reputation for the *Waffen-SS*. Initially, the *SS-Totenkopf-Division* and *Polize-Division* were a part of the reserves. Hitler sent both the *LSSAH* and the *Reich* to fight the short war against Yugoslavia in April 1941.

In the early morning hours of 22 June 1941, Hitler ordered 139 divisions to invade the Soviet Union. The *Totenkopf* was attached to Army Group North, the *Reich* to Army Group Center and the *LSSAH* and the *Wiking* to Army Group South. The new *SS-Division "Nord"* division was sent to Finland. At the beginning of the eastern campaign, every *Waffen-SS* unit participated in the fighting. The *Wiking's* first combat was near Tarnopol on 29 June, while the *LSAAH* fought in the unsuccessful breakthrough into the Crimea. The *Reich* was heavily engaged at Minsk and Smolensk, and Hausser lost an eye in battle some thirty kilometers from Moscow. The *Totenkopf* was first put into action near Lake Ilmen on 6 July.

The Soviet winter offensive in 1941/42 surprised the Germans, who were ill-equipped and unprepared for such an offensive. Many formations were cut off in "pockets". The most notable such pocket was at Demjansk, where six divisions, including the *Totenkopf*, were cut off. The Division sustained such heavy losses that it was renamed *Kampfgruppe Eicke*. In the winter offensive, the hardest hit was the *SS-Infanterie-Regiment "Der Führer"*, which was left with only 35 men ready for battle.

In March 1942, the *Reich* was withdrawn to France to rest and refit and the *Leibstandarte* followed in June. In May, the *Reich* was renamed as SS-Division *Das Reich*. The *Totenkopf* remained in Russia until October, when it was also withdrawn. Hitler noted the high combat value and reliability of the *SS* troops, and decided to militarily strengthen them, refitting some of the divisions with a strong tank component. These were then reformed as *SS-Panzer-Grenadier Divisionen*. The *Wiking* received reinforcements and remained in its position on the Mius River. In July 1942, the *Wiking* participated in Operation "Blau", breaking through with Army Group A toward the oil fields in the Caucasus Mountains. The Soviet counterattack in the winter of 1942 was disastrous for the Germans. The *6. Armee* was destroyed at Stalingrad and other German forces faced the danger of encirclement in the Caucasus Mountains. The *Wiking* held open the withdrawal route through Rostov. When the Soviet attacks ceased, the *Wiking* held the same position as in 1941, behind the Mius River However, at that time, it was substantially weakened and in need of reinforcements. From December 1942 to June 1943, new *Waffen-SS* divisions were formed: the *SS-Panzer-Grenadier-Division "Hohenstaufen"*, *SS-Panzer-Grenadier-Division "Karl der Große"* (later redesignated *"Frundsberg"*), the *SS-Panzer-Grenadier-Freiwilligen-Division "Nordland"* and the *SS-Panzer-Grenadier-Division "Hitlerjugend"*, thereby bringing the total number of *SS* troops to 200,000. However, none of these units would be battle-ready before the end of 1943.

Eventually the above named divisions were redesignated as follows: *1. SS-Panzer-Division "Leibstandarte SS Adolf Hitler"*, *2. SS-Panzer-Division "Das Reich"*, *3. SS-Panzer-Division "Totenkopf"*, *5. SS-Panzer-Division "Wiking"*, *9. SS-Panzer-Division "Hohenstaufen"*, *10. SS-Panzer-Division "Frundsberg"*, *11. SS-Freiwilligen-Panzer-Grenadier-Division "Nordland"* and *12 SS-Panzer-Division "Hitlerjugend"*. By the end of the war, a total of 38 *SS* divisions had been formed, of which 14 included armored elements.

In January 1943, the newly formed *SS-Panzer-Korps* with the *Leibstandarte* and the *Das Reich*, commanded by Paul Hausser, was sent to defend Kharkov with direct orders not to surrender the city. Under strong pressure from the Third Soviet Tank Army, Hauser requested the withdrawal of the *Leibstandarte* from the city on 13 February. Although Hitler denied this request, two days later Hausser withdrew from Kharkov along the only remaining road. Hitler ordered Hausser to be shot. However, von Manstein, with the *SS Panzerkorps* and the *Totenkopf* Division, succeeded in halting the Soviet penetration and Kharkov was retaken. On 18 March, the German High Command claimed the deaths of 50,000 Russian soldiers and the capture of another 20,000 during Manstein's counterattack. Hitler promptly forgot his previous command to execute Hausser.

The spring mud halted the operation, and von Manstein requested five weeks for his troops to rest and refit. His intent was to continue the breakthrough in early May, and to destroy the salient near Kursk. Hitler postponed the operation, instead awaiting the arrival of reinforcement in the form of new *Tiger* and *Panther* tanks. The *SS Panzer-Grenadier* Divisions *Leibstandarte*, *Das Reich* and *Totenkopf* each received one tank battalion, reinforced with one company of *Tiger* tanks. The new *I. SS-Panzer-Korps "Leibstandarte SS Adolf Hitler"* was also formed, under the command of Josef "Sepp" Dietrich. The core formation was the (at the time) *1. SS-Panzer-Grenadier-Division "Leibstandarte SS Adolf Hitler"*. Paul Hausser's Corps, with the *Das Reich* and *Totenkopf* divisions, was renamed as the *II. SS-Panzer-Korps*.

On July 5 1943, the largest battle of World War II began under the codename "*Operations Zitadelle*", with the participation of over 2 million German and Russian soldiers and 6,000 tanks. The *SS* divisions participated in the massive armored battles and fought well. In response to the Allied landings on Sicily as well as the Soviet attacks from the north that threatened to encircle Model's *9. Armee*, Hitler called off "*Operations Zitadelle*" on 17 July. The *Leibstandarte* left for Italy to reinforce the German forces there. The Soviet counterattack forced the German troops to retreat, and the *Das Reich*, the *Totenkopf* and the *Wiking* were sent to stop them before Kharkov. Heavily pressured on three sides, they were forced to retreat toward the Dnieper River on 22 August. The *Wiking* was sent to the Balkans to rest and refit, and the *Totenkopf* was sent as a reserve to an area near Dnepropetrovsk. The *LSSAH* became a full *SS-Panzer-Division* with the formation of its *panzerregiment* that included almost 200 *Panther* and *Pz.Kfw. IV* tanks. Refitted and reinforced, it was to take over the defense of Kiev. However, it remained on the Dnieper River due to the loss of the city on 7 November. The new Soviet breakthrough across the Dnieper River north of Kiev was halted in a counterattack by the *Das Reich* near Fastov. On 12 December, the *Totenkopf* and two *Heer* armored divisions counterattacked with the *LVII. Panzerkorps* at Krivoi Rog, where the Soviet advance was halted. Despite being reinforced by the *LSSAH* division, they could not push the Russians back across the Dnieper.

In anticipation of its new *Panzer-Abteilung*, armed with *Panthers* that were in training in France, the *Wiking* was sent to Cherkassy. The position of the Eastern Front eroded dramatically with the Soviet offensive across the Ukraine at the end of the year. In January, the *Wiking* Division was trapped in the

Korsun-Cherkassy pocket. It succeeded in breaking through, but lost one-third of its men and all its heavy weapons and vehicles in the process. One month later, the Soviet attack reached the *Leibstandarte* and what was left of the *Das Reich*, encircling them at Kamenets Podolsky. These units had to be rescued by the *Hohenstaufen* and the *Frundsberg*.

In the spring of 1944, the battered *SS* divisions were sent west, where they refitted in anticipation of the expected Anglo-American invasion. The *Hohenstaufen* and the *Frundsberg* were sent to Poland. The *Nordland* led the difficult defensive fighting, retreating from Leningrad toward Narwa. The *Wiking* was sent to Kowel to rest and refit, but was encircled in March in a surprise Soviet local attack. With the assistance of the *5. Panzer-Division* and the just-arrived *II./SS-Panzer-Regiment 5*, the encirclement was broken and Kowel was retained. At one point, the *Totenkopf* led the defensive battle on the Romanian border and withdrew to the central sector of the front.

In the summer of 1944, the long anticipated battle began. At the time of the Normandy landings, the *LSSAH* was in Belgium, the *Das Reich* was near the Spanish border and the *Hitlerjugend* was near Paris. The *Hitlerjugend* was immediately sent to attack, and was quickly followed by the *Das Reich*. By 29 June, the *Hohenstaufen* and *Frundsberg* had also arrived from Poland. The *LSSAH* was in reserve until 11 July, when it was pushed into battle. The British and Canadians launched major offensives on 12 and 26 June and 18 July, however those attacks were halted by strong German resistance. Concrete results were seen only with the arrival of the American armored divisions on 25 July. With the British tanks in the lead, and the Americans on the flanks, the Allies began to force the German forces toward the pocket at Falaise. The German counterattack toward Avranches came too late and achieved little. The Americans anticipated the new counterattack on 6 August near Mortain by the *LSSAH*, *Das Reich*, the *17 SS-Panzergrenadier-Division "Götz von Berlichingen"* and the *116. Panzer-Division*, and quickly stopped it. Facing the threat of encirclement of significant German forces on 15 August, the command to retreat was given. The *LSSAH*, the *Frundsberg* and the *Gotz von Berlichingen* succeeded in retreating with substantial losses, and were left virtually without any of their heavy armament. The *Das Reich*, the *Hohenstaufen* and the *Hitlerjugend* remained north of the pocket. However, due to the great losses endured, they too were forced to retreat.

In October, 1944, the greatest Soviet offensive so far in the war was halted before Warsaw with the assistance of the *Wiking* and the *Totenkopf*. This offensive led to the loss of virtually half a million German soldiers. The lull on the battlefront permitted the release of these two divisions into reserves.

The *Frundsberg* was sent near Arnhem to rest and refit while the *Hohenstaufen* was on the other side of the Rhine River in Germany. The Allies launched the airborne operation "Market Garden", with the intent of taking the bridges around Arnhem. Not being aware of the presence of the *SS Panzer Divisions*, the British Airborne dropped among them and was destroyed in two weeks. Assuming that the Allies were weakened by this failed operation, Hitler decided to hit through the Ardennes and take the port of Antwerp. He planned to cut off the British and Canadians and repeat Dunkirk. Though there was little chance for success, this offensive was launched on 16 December 1944. Thanks to the well-hidden preparations, the German attack surprised the Allies. The *LSSAH* and the *Hitlerjugend* were in the first line of attack, with the *Das Reich*

and the *Hohenstaufen* in the second line. The *Leibstandarte* succeeded in breaking through the Allied position, and penetrated about 30 kilometres before running out of fuel. The *Hitlerjugend* achieved only partial success. Their attempts to take Bastogne failed and they were forced to quickly retreat. The *Das Reich* and the *Hohenstaufen* were thrown into battle earlier than planned and had better success in their breakthrough. However, they met the same fate: strong resistance and a lack of fuel that ended their attack. The remnants of these two divisions retreated back to their initial positions.

With the arrival of the New Year, and in anticipation of renewed Allied offensives, the situation on all fronts was desperate. The Soviets entered Hungary and collected their forces at the Vistula River for the final offensive. The Western Allies were at the German border, preparing to cross the Rhine. The failed attack through the Ardennes had spent the last of the significant German reserves, both in terms of men and armor. In mid-December, the Soviets in Budapest besieged the *SS* cavalry divisions *8. Kavallerie-Division "Florian Geyer"* and *22. SS-Freiwilligen-Kavallerie-Division "Maria Theresa"*. Hitler's intent was to protect the Hungarian oil fields and to re-enter Budapest. The *Wiking* and *Totenkopf* were transferred from Poland to Hungary. The *IV. SS-Panzer-Korps* was the only reserve left behind the Vistula River. When the Soviets attacked, the front before them fell apart and they did not stop until they reached the Oder.

Though Germany faced attacks from two sides, Hitler sent his best units to Hungary. The deployment of the *6. SS-Panzer Armee* near Balaton Lake with the *LSSAH*, the *Hitlerjugend*, the *Hohenstaufen* and the *SS-Panzer-Grenadier-Division "Reichsführer SS"* that had arrived from Italy, was his final attempt. It was not successful. The failure of the *SS* units in Hungary had a disheartening effect on Hitler, who had expected these troops to do the impossible. He accused Dietrich and his subordinates of treason and forbade the *SS* units to wear their cuff bands. Under Allied pressure, the *SS* troops retreated towards the *Reich*, loyally fighting to the very end. The *Das Reich*, the *Wiking* and the *Frundsberg* surrendered in Czechoslovakia, the *Nordland* surrendered in Berlin, and the *LSSAH*, the *Totenkopf*, the *Hohenstaufen* and the *Hitlerjugend* laid down their arms in Austria.

During World War II, about 180,000 *Waffen-SS* soldiers were killed in action, 400,000 were wounded and 70,000 were listed as missing. It is interesting to note that 57 percent of the composition of the *SS* formations were non-Germans; Flemings, Waloons, Dutchmen, Danes, Finns, Norwegians, Italians, Frenchmen, Ukrainians, Latvians, Estonians, Romanians and Croats who fought within these units with their own distinctive insignia. Among them, many were decorated with the highest German awards. After the war, many were brought before the courts in their own countries, and convicted with the harshest sentences.

INTRODUCTION

The *"Leibstandarte SS Adolf Hitler"* (*"LSSAH"*) in France 1940 was a fully motorized unit. This photograph shows *SS* riflemen from the motorcycle battalion. Of interest is the fact that the wartime censor has removed all tactical markings from the motorcycle-sidecar combination (white areas on the sidecar and licence plate).

SS-Division "Wiking" Panzer crew stand on top of their new PzKpfw III Ausf J, Russia 1942. The division can be identified by the wheel-shaped swastika displayed on vehicles. Note also the wear of camouflage uniform articles. The Waffen-SS was a pioneer in this aspect of field clothing.

The "LSSAH" in Greece, 1941. This photograph shows heavy 150 mm howitzers (15cm sFH 36) of the SS-Artillerie-Regiment.

A 7.62cm PaK 36(r) self-propelled antitank gun of the SS–Panzerjäger–Abteilung "Wiking" in the Crimea, 1942.

"LSSAH" Panzergrenadiere advance with the support of a *PzKpfw IV Ausf G* during the battle for Kharkov, early 1943.

Generaloberst Guderian pays a visit to the *"LSSAH"* to inspect its new *Tigers*, spring 1943.

"Wiking" Panzergrenadiere in an *SdKfz 250 Neu* command APC in the summer of 1944.

In the battle of Kursk during the summer of 1943, the *"LSSAH"*, *"Das Reich"*, *"Totenkopf"* and *"Wiking"* were *Panzergrenadier–Divisionen*, and each had a battalion of tanks and a battalion of armored personnel carriers (APC's). In this instance an *SdKfz 251/10 Ausf C.*

An SS Panzer unit, equipped with captured American Shermans, advances along a road near the Rhine, January 1945.

ZHITOMIR - BERDICHEW
December 1943 - January 1944

In early November 1943, the Soviet High Command launched a massive offensive to seize Kiev in the Ukraine. Hitler decided to transfer the premier *Waffen-SS Panzer* formation, the *1. SS-Panzer-Division "Leibstandarte SS Adolf Hitler"* (*"LSSAH"*), from northern Italy. It was to help defend Kiev. The movement of the most powerful German *Panzer* division included 20,000 soldiers and almost 5,000 vehicles. Through virtually all of November, the temperature was above freezing, and the rains in the Ukraine turned the roads and fields into thick, muddy quagmires. This photograph shows a convoy of *"LSSAH"* vehicles slogging its way through the mud. APC's were mixed with transport vehicles in an effort to help pass through the mud. The *Opel "Blitz"* truck (box body) in the foreground is being towed by an *SdKfz 251/6* with a frame antenna. (Rottensteiner, Nov. 1943)

In the meantime, the Soviets took Kiev and the *"LSSAH"* arrived as reinforcements for the counterattack of the *XXXXVIII Panzer-Korps*, which was to have been under the veteran *Panzer* commander, *General der Panzertruppen* Hermann Balck. The planned attack was delayed due to the mud and the slow assembly of the *Panzer* units at Fastov. This photograph shows a convoy of *"LSSAH"* trucks on the "hard" muddy road. Snow chains have been mounted on the tires for greater mobility.

The trucks could only cross high-flowing rivers over bridges built by the pioneers. This photograph shows *SS-Panzer-Pioniere* raising a wooden bridge over a rain-swollen stream. In the background, APC "214" appears to be crossing the stream without difficulty.

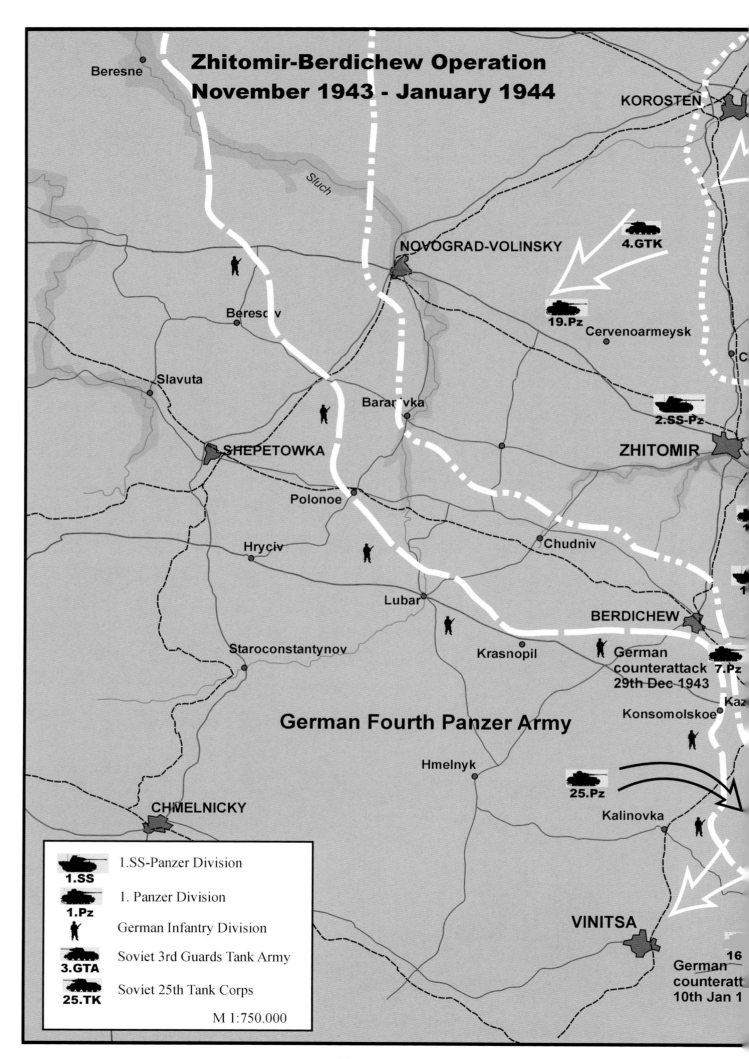

Zhitomir-Berdichew Operation
November 1943 - January 1944

Beresne

KOROSTEN

Sluch

NOVOGRAD-VOLINSKY

4.GTK

19.Pz

Berescv

Cervenoarmeysk

C

Slavuta

Bararvka

2.SS-Pz

ZHITOMIR

SHEPETOWKA

Polonoe

Chudniv

Hryciv

1

Lubar

BERDICHEW

Staroconstantynov

Krasnopil

German
counterattack   7.Pz
29th Dec 1943

Kaz

German Fourth Panzer Army

Konsomolskoe

Hmelnyk

25.Pz

Kalinovka

CHMELNICKY

VINITSA

16
German
counteratt
10th Jan 1

1.SS	1.SS-Panzer Division
1.Pz	1. Panzer Division
	German Infantry Division
3.GTA	Soviet 3rd Guards Tank Army
25.TK	Soviet 25th Tank Corps

M 1:750.000

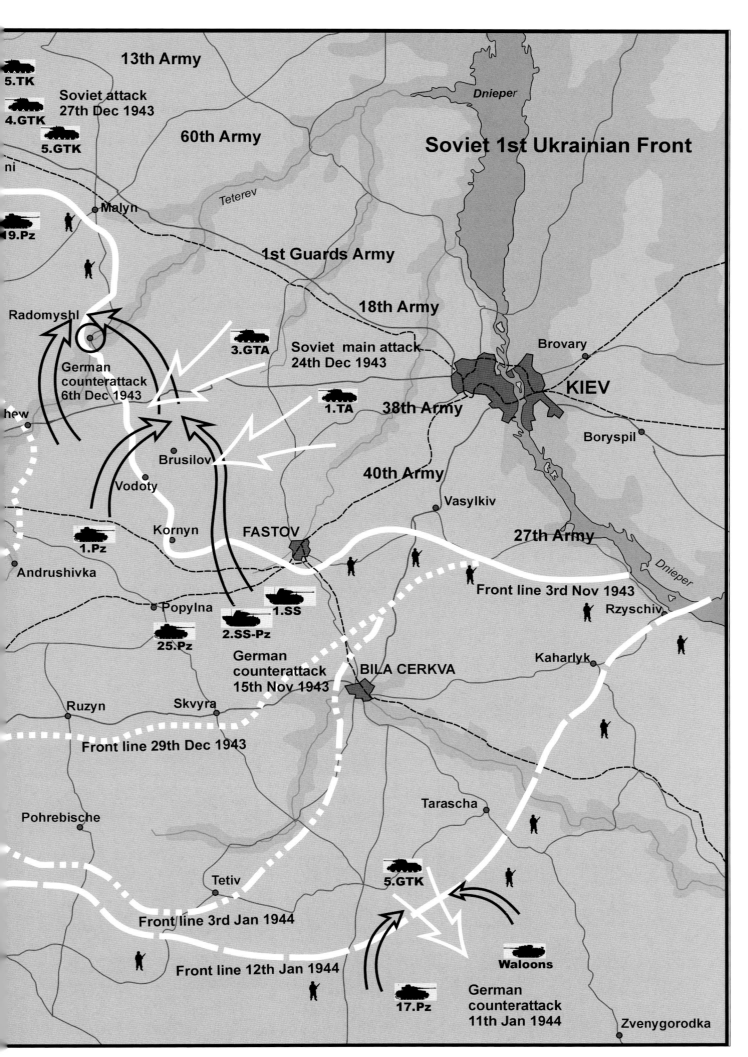

13

A convoy of *"LSSAH" Tigers* passes over an improvised wooden bridge during the fighting around Zhitomir. *SS-Panzer-Regiment 1.* was reinforced with 27 *Tigers* in its 13th Company. The first *Tiger* in the convoy has the number "S23", and the second "S24" (s - stands for *schwere* - heavy - *Panzer-Kompanie*). The company had two command tanks, "S04" and "S05", and 5 platoons with 5 tanks each. That means the *Tigers* in the photograph are the 3rd and 4th tanks in the 2nd platoon. (Rottensteiner, Nov. 1943)

13.s.SS-Pz.Kompanie "LSSAH", November 1943

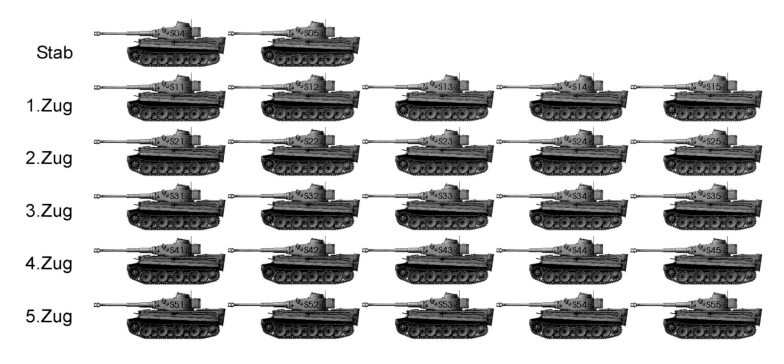

Due to their great fuel consumption, the *Tigers* had a cross-country range of about 60 kilometers, and only half of that in muddy terrain. As such, their battle usage depended heavily on the supply trucks. The truck in the photograph (*SS*-1693 29), stuck in the mud, belongs to the heavy company. The soldiers are unloading 200 liter fuel drums to lighten the truck before digging it out of the mud. (Rottensteiner, Nov. 1943)

The staff of the heavy company was equipped with light vehicles such as the *VW Kübelwagen*. Nine SS soldiers were able to pull the 700 kg vehicle out of the mud. (Rottensteiner, Nov. 1943)

The *VW Schwimmwagen* (SS-302098) was a light amphibious vehicle. Clearly visible on its side is the insignia of the *"LSSAH"* – a key inside a shield. *Panther* tanks can be seen in the background. (Rottensteiner, Nov. 1943)

As part of its armor complement, the *"Leibstandarte"* had an assault gun battalion (*SS-Sturmgeschutz–Abteilung 1.*) with three batteries, totalling 30 *StuG III's*. They were to reinforce the antitank defense of the division, but were used as tanks instead. This photograph shows a *StuG III* in its most dangerous role, the concealed hunter waiting for his prey. (Keimling, Nov. 1943)

This *SS-Panzergrenadier* heavy machine-gun nest is well dug into the loose soil. Visible in the photograph is the *MG42* heavy machine-gun, which had a rate of fire of 1,600 rounds per minute. The motorized battalion had 70-80 machine-guns, while the mechanized battalion had 110 *MG34* or *MG42* machine-guns. (Rottensteiner Nov. 1943)

The *"LSSAH"* had two regiments of motorized infantry, with three battalions each. They totalled about 6,500 men and about 1,000 vehicles. Each battalion had three companies of grenadiers and a support company armed with heavy weapons. Though the division was a prestigious formation, only the *III./SS-Panzer-Grenadier-Regiment 2* was mechanized. It had about 90 *SdKfz 251* APC's. In the photograph, the *Panzergrenadiere* wait to mount the transporters.

The *SS-Panzergrenadier* regiments had strong integral antitank and antiaircraft weapons. This photograph shows the crew of an antitank gun. With its low profile, it was hard to spot when dug in. The crew covered the top with canvas to mask the straight lines of its silhouette and to make the gun less recognizable. (Rottensteiner, Dec. 1943)

The strongest element of the *"LSSAH"* division, with 96 *Panthers*, was the *I. Panzer Abteilung*. It was organized into four companies, numbered from 1 to 4, each with 22 tanks. The headquarters had 3 tanks, and the reconnaissance platoon had another 5. The photograph shows a *Panther* tank of the *I./SS-Panzer-Regiment 1.* near Zhitomir. The rain shield over the binocular sight holes in the mantlet indicates that this vehicle is a late D variant. (Pachnicke, Dec. 1943)

Under the command of the *XXXXVIII. Panzer–Korps*, an impressive armored force was gathered together in November. It was used by von Manstein to take Zhitomir and prevent the Soviets from capturing the vital railway hubs of Berdichew, Kazatin and Korosten. The full-strength *"LSSAH"* and the weak 2. *SS-Panzer-Grenadier-Division "Das Reich"*, plus four *Heer Panzer-Divisionen*, formed the core of the 500-strong tank force. The *Panthers* of the *"LSSAH"* were the main striking force. Soviet losses included some 25,000 men, 300 artillery pieces, 1,200 antitank guns and 600 tanks. The photograph shows a convoy of *SS Panthers*. The first in the convoy appears to be numbered "353". (Pachnicke, Dec. 1943)

21

A convoy of "*LSSAH*" *Panthers* is on the march near Zhitomir and Berdichew. With the frozen ground and the first snow falling in December, the tanks had virtually unlimited movement possibilities. However, due to the equipment losses in November, their offensive capacity was significantly reduced. *SS Panzer-Regiment 1* was reduced to only three companies; one each of *PzKfw. V (Panthers)*, *PzKfw. VI (Tigers)* and *PzKfw.IV's*, totalling about 40 tanks. (Pachnicke, Dec. 1943)

A group of *SS-Panzergrenadiere* show the photographer their battle tactics in a mock attack. From May 1943, the assault guns and medium tanks were fitted with *"Schürzen"* (aprons) steel plates as sideskirts. However, in the numerous photographs, as in this one, taken in November and December, the *StuG III's* from the *"LSSAH"* did not have sideskirts. Instead, its crew protected the weaker sides with spare track links. (Ahrens, Dec. 1943)

Training of *SS-Panzer-Pioniere* in clearing roads of wooden antitank mines. The German tactics stressed close cooperation between all combat arms. The combat engineers cleared passages through the minefields, while the assault guns provided cover. (Ahrens, Dec. 1943)

The loader in a *StuG* was also the machine-gunner. He was protected by a metal shield, through which the *MG34* machine-gun could fire. Note the spare track links and three ammunition boxes, each of which could hold 300 rounds of 7.92 mm ammunition. (Ahrens, Dec. 1943)

Another photograph of the *StuG* crew and *SS-Panzergrenadiere*. The commander of the *StuG*, an *SS-Untersturmführer* (2nd Lieutenant), studies the map. The gunner has a reversible hood on his head, fastened around the neck with a cloth tape. The hood efficiently protected the lower half of the face. To maintain maximum hearing, the hood has round ear openings. (Ahrens, Dec 1943)

Well-coated with white winter paint, and due to its low height of only 2.16 meters, the *StuG III* was hard to spot in deep snow. The Soviets issued special instructions for combatting these weapons. A convoy of *StuG's* awaits departure for battle near Zhitomir. The photograph also shows a *2cm Flak* gun mounted on an *SdKfz 10/4* halftrack.

This *Panther Ausf. D*, number "345", from the *"LSSAH"* division is still painted with the base sand color (*sandgelb*). A number of the *Panthers* did not receive a coat of whitewash or the *Zimmerit* protective coating against magnetic charges. (Büschel, Jan. 1944)

At full strength *II./SS Panzer-Regiment 1*, had 96 *PzKpfw IV* medium tanks in four companies, numbered 5-8. In January, the *"LSSAH"* had only 20 of these tanks ready for action, and just as many in the repair shop. The battle in the Ukraine took on a defensive character, where the tanks were used only in small local counterattacks. In the photograph, tank "530" supports the infantry in defense. The tank crews, particularly in the *SS Panzer* divisions, were happy to wear the thick leather jackets and coats – originally designed for *U-Boot* crews, which offered some protection against burning fuel and provided warmth in the unheated tanks. (Büschel, Jan. 1944)

Infantry clear away the snow and ice before a convoy of *PzKpfw IV* tanks. It is very likely that this convoy included wheeled vehicles, as this type of snow did not present a problem for the tanks - although deep snow and ice did.

The medium *PzKpfw IV* tank was, in German hands, an equal rival to the excellent Soviet T-34 tanks armed with 76 mm guns. Against this tank, its 75 mm gun was effective at distances of up to 1,500 meters. The crews of the *PzKpfw IV* tanks frequently strengthened the weak 50 mm turret armor and 80 mm hull armor with spare track links. From May 1943, the assault guns and medium tanks were fitted with the *Schürzen* sideskirts.

A group of *SS* grenadiers rest in the winter sun while awaiting further orders. They are wearing the 1943 pattern parka and trousers with the white side out and the camouflage side in. The helmet was painted in white to blend in with the landscape.(Rottensteiner, Jan. 1944)

A moment of rest with a bottle of wine for the *SS-Panzergrenadier* in the APC, and the maintenance mechanic. The mechanic wears interesting one-piece camouflage overalls with a breast pocket. In collecting circles these one-piece camouflage coveralls are considered to be among the rarest *Waffen-SS* uniform items and are priced acordingly. (Rottensteiner, Jan. 1944)

A destroyed Model 1943 Soviet T-34. The *Panthers* could destroy these tanks at distances up to 3,000 meters. At a distance of 2,000 meters, an average of four rounds was required, while at a distance of 1,000 meters, usually two rounds were sufficient to destroy a T-34. At least four penetrations can be seen in the picture. (Büschel, Jan, 1944)

SS soldiers look over a destroyed Soviet SU-152 heavy assault gun, armed with a 152 mm gun-howitzer. Because its powerful gun could destroy the heavy German *Tiger* and medium *Panther* tanks, it was nicknamed the "Animal Killer". Its greatest tactical disadvantage was its firing rate of only two rounds a minute. The German gun penetrated the 75 mm thick hull armor plate and caused an internal ammunition explosion that destroyed the SU-152. (Pachnicke, Jan. 1944)

The *"Leibstandarte"* and the *1. Panzer-Division* launched an attack on Radomyschl on 19 December. At first, the attack went well, but it then ran into a huge belt of antitank guns. The attack got bogged down, and the *"LSSAH"* division brought its heavy 88mm *Flak* guns forward to destroy the enemy guns. (Pachnicke, Dec. 1943)

The 88mm *Flak 36* heavy antiaircraft gun was often used in the direct-fire antitank role and for delivering indirect fire as well, which is why it had a shield for the crew and extra sights for engaging ground targets. The gun was manned by a commander and a detachment of nine men. The *SS-Flak-Ateilung 1/"LSSAH"* had three heavy batteries with a total of 12 such guns. Unlike the previous photograph, in which the gun was emplaced, this one is firing directly from its trailer.

An 88mm *Flak 37* in position. Around New Years Day 1944, the tanks and *Flak* halted several breakthroughs through the lines of the *"LSSAH"*. On 29 December alone, 59 Soviet tanks were destroyed, including at least a dozen destroyed by *Flak* guns. Note the camouflage net on the gun shield. (Möbius, Jan. 1944)

A wide range of ammunition was produced for the 88mm gun, including the *Pzgr 40* armor-piercing round. At a distance of 2,000 meters, it could penetrate armor up to 110mm thick, and was powerful enough to destroy a T-34 tank at even greater distances. The semi-automatic breech greatly eased the loading process. Loader 2 is handing a round to Loader 1.

A group of *"LSSAH"* soldiers has a smoke break. On the right is an *SS-Rottenführer* (Corporal) in the M1936 service tunic. His rank insignia include the braid silver stripe on the collar patch and two V stripes on the left sleeve under the eagle. The Iron Cross 1st Class and the infantry assault badge are attached to the left pocket. The Iron Cross 2nd Class ribbon is slipped through a buttonhole. (Adendorf, Feb. 1944)

In this interesting photograph, a soldier prepares uniforms for cleaning in the large machine partially visible behind him. All the uniforms belong to non-commissioned officers. Cuff titles recognizable on the uniforms are: *"Das Reich", "Deutschland", "Adolf Hitler"* and *"Legion Flanders"*. (Adendorf, Feb. 1944)

"LSSAH" crews, likely from the reconnaissance battalion, during a short break. Among the numerous Schwimmwagen, is a 5 cm PaK 38 antitank gun mounted on a partially armored 1–ton SdKfz 10.

A group of *"LSSAH"* soldiers eats during a break. The soldier closest to the camera has the *SS* runes on his helmet. In the background is a *StuG III*. (Pachnicke, Jan. 1944)

The *SdKfz 236* was issued to the reconnaissance units of *Panzer* and *Panzergrenadier* divisions, as well as Corps and Army headquarters. A large frame antenna and a telescope mast antenna were provided for long-range communications. The only armament was the *MG 34*. The *SS-Oberscharführer* (Staff Sergeant) from the *"Leibstandarte"* receives a radio message and records it in the official logbook. (Pachnicke, Jan. 1944)

The *SS-Panzer-Aufklarungs Abteilung 1* (Armored Reconnaissance Battalion) was the eyes and ears of the *"LSSAH"* division. The best officers served in it, and they were expected to assess the situation in the field and report back to headquarters. The battalion was well equipped with fast and mobile *SdKfz 250* and *SdKfz 251* APC's. This photograph shows a heavy, cross-country *Panzerfunkwagen SdKfz 263* radio car and an APC. (Pachnicke, Jan. 1944)

SS-Standartenführer (Colonel) Otto Baum, commander of *SS-Panzer-Grenadierregiment "Totenkopf"*, later became the commander of *"Das Reich"*. (Adendorf, Feb. 1944)

1./SS-Sturmgeschütz-Abteilung 1 "LSSAH", February 1944

1. Kompanie

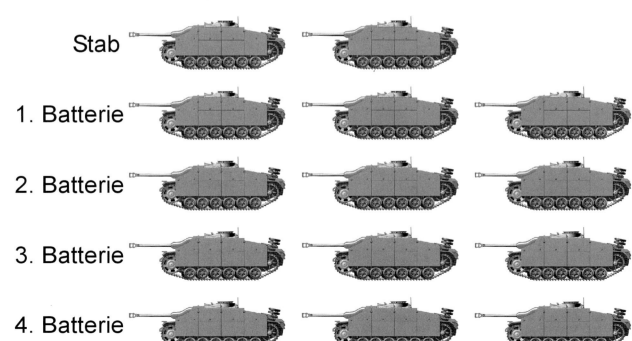

Stab

1. Batterie

2. Batterie

3. Batterie

4. Batterie

In early January, the "LSSAH" was pulled out of the line near Berdichew and moved north to try to close the gap between the *XXXXVIII Panzer-Korps* and the *LIX Korps*. The Division's maintenance company succeeded in repairing a number of damaged vehicles, bringing the available number to 4 *Tigers*, 17 *Panthers*, 8 *PzKpfw IV's*, 15 *StuG III's* and 4 self-propelled antitank guns. The Division's *Kampfgruppen* (battle groups) spent three weeks eliminating small Soviet breakthroughs that penetrated the German line. The photograph shows one of the *Kampfgruppen*. (Pachnicke, Jan. 1944)

Kampfgruppen were created by combining elements from divisional formations, according to the missions they had to execute. The tactics of these *Kampfgruppen* are still studied today in many military academies. The photograph shows *SS-Panzergrenadiere* and a tank from the *"LSSAH"* division. However, tanks of the *Wehrmacht* are also present. If one focuses on the *Tiger*, it becomes apparent that its number is "200", not a *Waffen-SS* number at that time. (Pachnicke, Jan. 1944)

This *Kampfgruppe* is comprised of *Tigers*, *Panthers*, *PzKpfw IV*'s, *StuG III*'s, and *Hummel* and *Wespe* self-propelled artillery. Among them is at least one *PzKpfw III* command tank. It appears that there are about thirty armored vehicles and several companies of SS-*Panzergrenadiere*. Visible, at the left of the photograph, are a trailer and part of an *SdKfz. 10/4* antiaircraft halftrack. (Pachnicke, Jan. 1944)

During its occupation duties in northern Italy, the *"LSSAH"* managed to acquire a Fiat 665 truck and an excellent four-wheel drive Fiat 666 NM. This photograph shows one of the Fiat trucks, with the clearly visible insignias of the *"LSSAH"* and the heavy tank company. Soldiers are removing 200 liter barrels from the truck. Next to the truck are a *StuG III*, and *Wespe* and *Hummel* self-propelled howitzers, which were used by the *Kampfgruppe* as direct fire support. (Pachnicke, Jan. 1944)

A group of *SS-Panzergrenadiere* prepares to mount a *Panther* tank, which carries the German flag for easy recognition from the air. Note the spare road wheel on the *Panther*. (Pachnicke, Jan. 1944)

Germany's most successful and famous tank commander, *SS-Hauptsturmführer* (Captain) Michael Wittmann, poses with his crew in front of his *Tiger* "S04". The 88 "kill rings" were painted for a decoration ceremony for him and his crew. Wittmann received the *Eichenlaub* (Oakleaves) to the Knight's Cross. Shown in the photograph are (left to right) Wittmann, *SS-Rottenführer* Bobby Woll, *SS-Panzerschütze* Werner Irrgang, *SS-Panzerschütze* Sepp Rössner and *SS-Sturmmann* Eugen Schmidt. (Büschel, Feb. 1944)

This group of *SS-Panzergrenadiere* wears winter caps made of rabbit fur as part of their winter uniforms. The only *SS* insignia is the steel belt buckle. In other photographs, some of them have *SS* regulation eagles pinned to the front of the fur headgear. (Pachnicke, Jan. 1943)

"LSSAH" assault guns await the order to attack. The spacing between the vehicles should not be less than 100 meters. If enemy artillery opened fire, only a portion of the formation would be hit. The *StuGs* in the second row cover the lead vehicles with their guns. (Rottensteiner, Jan. 1944)

This enemy 37 mm antiaircraft battery was taken in a surprise attack across open terrain. (Büschel, Jan. 1943)

The repair of this *StuG* in the open field was carried out under very difficult weather conditions. The only protection from the cold steppe wind was provided by a wall built from blocks of snow.

An *"LSSAH"* *Wespe* (Wasp) self-propelled artillery gun with its crew. Its main weapon was the 105 mm *leFH18M* light field howitzer. The *Wespe* was issued to the self-propelled detachments of the *Panzerartillerie* regiments in the *Panzer* and *Panzergrenadier* divisions. An *SS-Panzer-Artillerie-Regiment* had four artillery battalions, each with three batteries. The armored battalion had two light batteries of *Wespe* and one heavy battery of *Hummel* self-propelled guns. Each battery had six guns. At the end of 1943 *"LSSAH"* had its 2nd battalion equipped with armored artillery, *Das Reich* the 3rd battalion and *Totenkopf* the 1st battalion in the *SS-Panzerartillerie-Regiment*. (Rottensteiner, Jan. 1944)

The *Hummel* (Bumblebee) was a self-propelled artillery vehicle, armed with a 150 mm *sFH18/1* howitzer mounted on a hybrid *PzKpfw III/IV* chassis. While, initially, each *SS-Panzer-Division* had only six *Hummeln*, later some received a second battery.

SS Hummeln drive at full speed. The letter A indicates that this is the first *Hummel* battery, B and C are *Wespe* batteries. The wide, so-called *Ostkette* tracks ("Eastern tracks") were used in Russia because of the poor weather and terrain. The bolted-on track extenders were often shed during turns or manoeuvres at high speed or in rough terrain, because extra pressure was exerted on the outer edges of the tracks.

A *Panzer* division carried with it 200 tons of ammunition for its artillery. This quantity was theoretically sufficient for one week of sustained operations. Whenever possible, the empty ammo boxes and expended copper casings were collected and sent back to Germany by rail. This photograph shows the unloading of boxes and casings from a *Maultier* halftrack. Note the difference between the 105 and 150 mm casings. (Möbius, March 1944)

Although the *Hummel's* height (more than three meters) and its thin armor were its significant tactical disadvantages, having six such vehicles was of immense importance to a division. For a *Panzer* division, it was a priority to camouflage its *Hummeln*. For this reason, photographs where they are not whitewashed or painted white during winter are very rare. Even this vehicle's wheels are whitewashed.

The *Panzerjäger* battalion of an *SS-Panzer-Division* had three companies of antitank guns. One or two companies had self-propelled antitank guns, such as the *Marder II* shown in the photograph. The 75 mm *Pak 40/2* antitank gun, which could penetrate the armor of Soviet medium tanks, was mounted on a high, lightly-armored superstructure that offered minimum protection. For that reason, the *Marders* should not have been used in the role of tanks. However, due to the high number of tank losses, the *Marders* were used as replacements. For example, on 7 January 1944, the *"LSSAH"* had at its disposal 4 *Tigers*, 8 *Panthers*, 11 *StuG's*, plus 4 *Marders* and 4 towed antitank guns that were used as tanks!

During 1943, the *"LSSAH"* received 20 self-propelled 75 mm antitank guns on the Czech tank chassis, known as the *Marder III Ausf. H*. These guns were used during the occupation of Italy in September 1944. While it is difficult to determine just how many of these guns went to the Eastern Front as part of *1./SS-Panzerjäger-Abteilung 1.*, they were certainly seen there. (Geller, Apr. 1944)

Separate *SS–Werfer–Abteilung 502*, a rocket-launcher battalion of three batteries, was attached to the *"Das Reich"* in November 1943. The *2./SS–Werfer–Abteilung 502* was shipped to France in January 1943, while the other two batteries remained as *SS–Werfergruppe Krosta* as part of the *"Das Reich" Kampfgruppe*. The photograph shows the rocket launchers in position. The blackened snow shows that they had recently fired. The *SdKfz 11/1* halftracks served as prime movers for the rockets. (Möbius, Jan. 1944)

A 15 cm Nebelwerfer 41 and its SS crew. The Nebelwerfers were difficult to conceal in action because of their heavy backblast, and the long, smoky trails left by the rockets along their trajectories. For these reasons, the towing vehicles had to be nearby so that they could quickly move the battery to a new position.

The *"LSSAH"*, as well as *"Das Reich"*, occasionally had an attached battery of *15 cm Nebelwerfers 41*. The six rockets from each launcher were fired singly at two-second intervals, meaning the battery of four launchers could fire 24 rockets in only 12 seconds, which was great firing power. This photograph shows the rocket battery from the *"LSSAH"* ready to fire. (Möbius, Jan. 1944)

An *SS* artilleryman from the *"LSSAH"* holds a 32 kilogram *15 cm Wurfgranate 41* rocket. The rocket's range was 7,000 meters.

The ready machine-gunner and the low angle of the barrels on the rocket launchers show that the enemy is very close. The relatively low weight of the launcher permitted the four-man crew to handle it easily.

The powerful blast of the rockets was visible from great distances, and allowed enemy observers to quickly pinpoint the battery's position. (Möbius, Jan. 1944)

In January and February, the *"LSSAH"* and *Kampgruppe "Das Reich"* primarily fought defensive engagements. Occasionally, smaller armored forces carried out local counterattacks, in which smaller Soviet forces were known to be encircled. Such pockets of resistance had to be quickly eliminated prior to the arrival of enemy reinforcements. Such a scenario would be feasible for this photograph, in which heavy cannons (15 cm) and rocket launchers are positioned close to each other. (Brockhausen, Feb. 1944)

A dramatic scene of evacuating the wounded. The *SdKfz 250/3* command APC serves as protection against enemy fire. It appears that its crew are assisting in caring for the wounded. (Rottensteiner, Jan. 1944)

After the wounded were evacuated from the front line, they received medical assistance and then were transported to field hospitals in light medical vehicles. (Rottensteiner, Jan. 1944)

SS troops used captured Soviet equipment, especially to replace their own losses. Very frequently, seized weapons were immediately used against their former owners. In the photograph, gunners from the *"LSSAH"* prepare to fire from a captured Soviet Model 1927 76 mm infantry gun. The large wheels provided extra protection for the crew. The Germans captured a large number of these guns. They went to the trouble of making their own ammunition for them, and even fitted them with German sights.

THE CHERKASSY POCKET
1 - 18 February 1944

By January 1944, the *5. SS-Panzer-Division"Wiking"*, though re-designated in October 1943 as an *SS-Panzer-Division*, still had not received its *Panther-Abteilung*. It had only 12 *PzKpfw III's*, 8 *PzKpfw IV's* and 4 *StuG III's* ready for action. In the photograph, the *"Wiking" Kampfgruppe* is ready for action on the southern banks of the Dnieper River. (Pachnicke, Jan. 1944)

Armored personnel carriers were never available in sufficient numbers and, therefore, tanks and assault guns frequently transported grenadiers, particularly in winter, when long marches through the snow were very difficult. Thus, they could quickly transport significant forces over greater distances. In the photograph, *StuG III* number "19" transports grenadiers of the *"Wiking"* division. (Pachnicke, Jan. 1944)

As seen on this *PzKpfw IV* driving across the snow covered steppe, between twenty and twenty-five grenadiers could stand on one vehicle. The best place for riding was on the engine deck, where the soldiers could warm their feet.

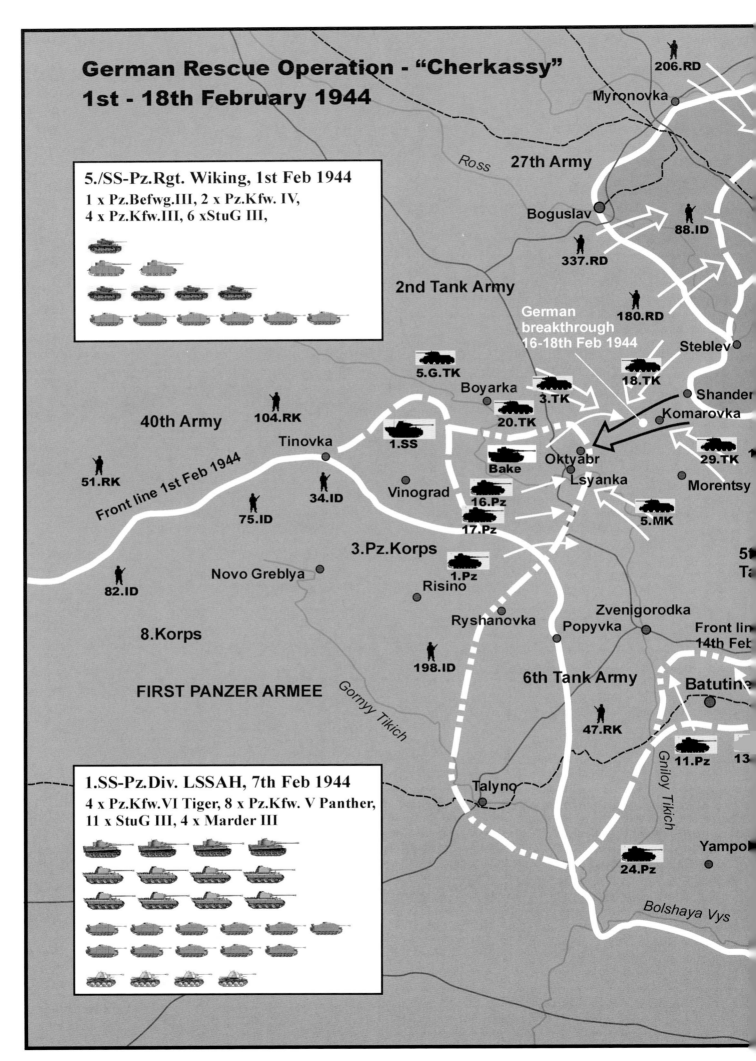

**German Rescue Operation - "Cherkassy"
1st - 18th February 1944**

5./SS-Pz.Rgt. Wiking, 1st Feb 1944
1 x Pz.Befwg.III, 2 x Pz.Kfw. IV,
4 x Pz.Kfw.III, 6 xStuG III,

206.RD

Myronovka

Ross **27th Army**

Boguslav

88.ID

337.RD

2nd Tank Army

180.RD

German
breakthrough
16-18th Feb 1944

Steblev

5.G.TK

Boyarka

3.TK

18.TK

Shander

Komarovka

40th Army

104.RK

20.TK

1.SS

29.TK

Tinovka

Oktyabr

Front line 1st Feb 1944

Bake

Lsyanka

Morentsy

51.RK

34.ID

Vinograd

16.Pz

5.MK

75.ID

17.Pz

3.Pz.Korps

1.Pz

Novo Greblya

Risino

Zvenigorodka

Front lin
14th Feb

8.Korps

82.ID

Ryshanovka

Popyvka

FIRST PANZER ARMEE

198.ID

6th Tank Army

Batutine

Gornyy Tikich

47.RK

11.Pz

13

1.SS-Pz.Div. LSSAH, 7th Feb 1944
4 x Pz.Kfw.VI Tiger, 8 x Pz.Kfw. V Panther,
11 x StuG III, 4 x Marder III

Talyno

Gniloy Tikich

24.Pz

Yampo

Bolshaya Vys

58

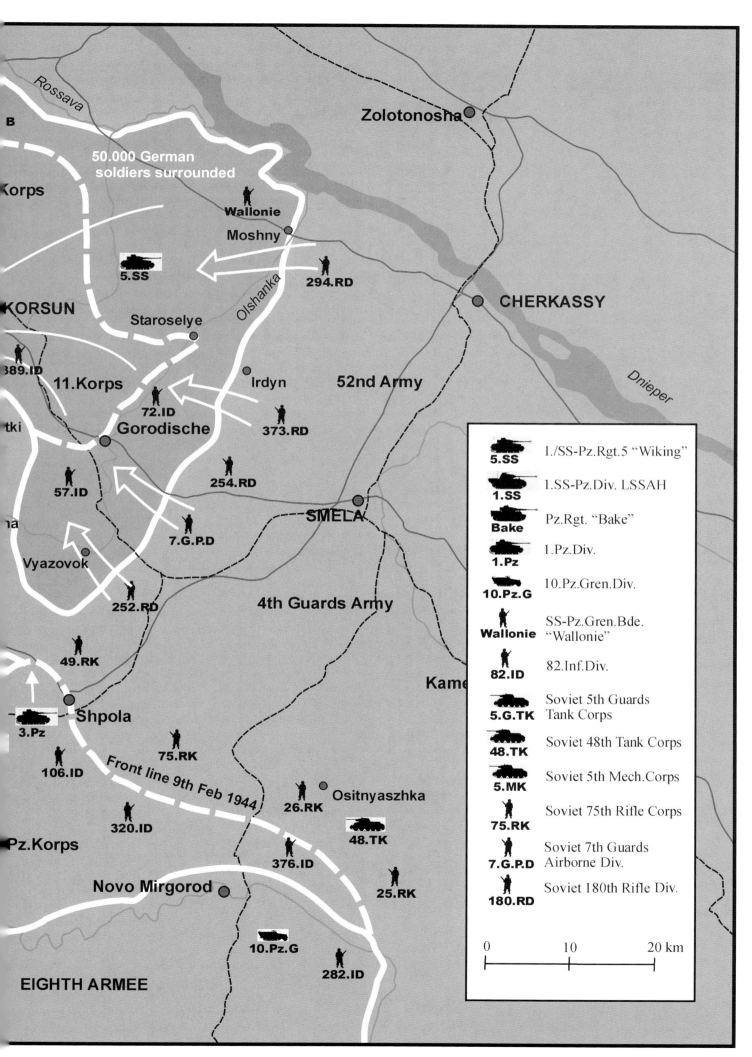

B

Rossava

Zolotonosha

Korps

50.000 German soldiers surrounded

Wallonie

Moshny

5.SS

294.RD

Olshanka

CHERKASSY

KORSUN

Staroselye

389.ID

11.Korps

Irdyn

52nd Army

Dnieper

tki

72.ID

Gorodische

373.RD

254.RD

57.ID

SMELA

na

7.G.P.D

Vyazovok

4th Guards Army

252.RD

Kame

49.RK

Shpola

3.Pz

75.RK

106.ID

Front line 9th Feb 1944

Ositnyaszhka

26.RK

320.ID

48.TK

376.ID

Novo Mirgorod

25.RK

Pz.Korps

10.Pz.G

EIGHT ARMEE

282.ID

5.SS	I./SS-Pz.Rgt.5 "Wiking"
1.SS	1.SS-Pz.Div. LSSAH
Bake	Pz.Rgt. "Bake"
1.Pz	1.Pz.Div.
10.Pz.G	10.Pz.Gren.Div.
Wallonie	SS-Pz.Gren.Bde. "Wallonie"
82.ID	82.Inf.Div.
5.G.TK	Soviet 5th Guards Tank Corps
48.TK	Soviet 48th Tank Corps
5.MK	Soviet 5th Mech.Corps
75.RK	Soviet 75th Rifle Corps
7.G.P.D	Soviet 7th Guards Airborne Div.
180.RD	Soviet 180th Rifle Div.

0   10   20 km

Heavily loaded with ammunition and weapons, these *SS-Panzergrenadiere* lie on the ground to partially lighten their load. It appears that this is the crew of an *SdKfz 251* APC. Note the two shovels and axe, used for digging into the frozen ground. (Adendorf, Feb. 1944)

Approximately 1,600 French and Belgian volunteers were already serving in German units on the Eastern Front, when several hundred new recruits were incorporated into the *Waffen-SS*. From the two groups, the *SS-Freiwilligen-Sturm-Brigade "Wallonien"* was formed, and then was placed under the command of the *5. SS-Panzer-Grenadier-Division "Wiking"* on 19 November 1943. The brigade consisted of three companies of infantry, a company of heavy weapons, an antitank company, an assault gun battery (with 11 guns), a platoon of engineers and a platoon of motorcyclists. All the units were fully motorized. The photograph shows a convoy of Walloon *StuG's* and mounted infantry. (Jarolim, Jan. 1944)

Suspecting the presence of antitank mines, the Walloons test the terrain in front of their vehicles. In November 1943, a cast gun mantlet was introduced on the *StuG* production line. Called the *Saukopfblende* (sow's head mantlet), it is clearly visible in these photographs. The Walloons were among the first troops to receive these *StuG's*. It is evident that these vehicles are brand new. Vehicles delivered in the winter were not painted in camouflage colors. They left the factory either painted in a sand color, or were temporarily coated with whitewash. (Jarolim, Jan. 1944)

Several weeks after these photographs were taken, the Walloons were encircled in what is known as the Korsun, or Cherkassy Pocket. They lost all their heavy equipment, and only 632 men managed to escape. (Jarolim, Jan. 1944)

View of a *StuG III* from the rear. The *Balkenkreuz* on the back is the only visible marking on the vehicle. Note the helmets that the crew hung on the rail at the back of the fighting compartment. They were too cumbersome to be stowed within the fighting compartment, (Jarolim, Jan. 1944)

It appears that the testing of the terrain and searching for antitank mines was not just an exercise for the camera. This *StuG* has lost its left track, probably due to a mine. Judging by the prepared cable, the crew appears to be preparing for a tow. (Jarolim, Jan. 1944)

This Walloon *MG 34* machine-gun crew is ready for every possibility, while the *StuG* crew prepares for towing. Note the two *M1941* ammunition boxes with 300 rounds each, one 50 round belt around the neck of the loader, and another with 50 rounds ready to be fired. (Jarolim, Jan. 1944)

Thanks primarily to the defensive efforts of the *"Totenkopf"* division, Krivoi Rog, the important supply and communication centre for *Heeresgruppe Sud*, remained in German hands until early February 1944. In these actions, its *Tigers* destroyed a large number of Soviet tanks. This photograph is most likely a *"Totenkopf" Tiger* with the new commander's cupola. The commander is carefully observing the battlefield while his crew repairs damage from the recent fighting. The track has been laid out in front of the vehicle to facilitate its remounting once the repairs are effected. (Pachnicke, Jan. 1944)

A photograph of the tank shown on page 64 from the other side. The crewmen are re-pairing one of the outer wheels. In the event that one of the wheels in the inner row was damaged, it was necessary to remove 5 or 6 wheels to get to it. This was a very difficult task, especially in times of bad weather. (Pachnicke, Jan. 1944)

This *SS-Unterscharführer* (Sergeant) tank commander wears the distinctive *SS*-pattern *Panzer* jacket. On his left sleeve is the *"Totenkopf"* cuff title. Note the headset with throat microphone so that his voice could be heard over gunfire or the noise of the engine. It is interesting to note that despite being assigned to the *"Totenkopf"* division this noncommissioned officer wears a standard *SS* collar tab as opposed to the *"Totenkopf"*-style collar tab unique to the division.

On the back of the photograph the author noticed that the photographer shot a battery of self-propelled *Wespe* howitzers from the *SS–Freiwilligen–Panzer–Grenadier–Bataillon "Narwa"*, which was composed of Estonian volunteers. They were attached to the *SS–Panzer–Grenadier–Division "Wiking"*, and served in its *"Westland"* Regiment. Like the Walloons, they suffered heavy losses in the Cherkassy Pocket. (Jarolim, Jan. 1944)

SS–Freiwillige (SS-volunteers), likely Walloons, man a *7.5 cm le.IG 18* light infantry gun. Issued to the support companies of infantry regiments, this was one of the most widely used guns in German service. The gun position in the photograph is well supplied with ammunition.

On 28 January 1944, two Soviet armored pincers closed in around two German corps, trapping 56,000 men in the so-called Cherkassy Pocket. Among them was the *5. SS-Panzer-Division "Wiking"*. Hitler ordered that the pocket be defended so that relief units could fight their way in. On 4 February, the *"LSSAH"*, the *16. Panzer-Division* and *17. Panzer-Division*, with *schweres Panzer Regiment "Bäke"* (47 *Panthers* and 34 *Tigers* from *schwere Panzer-Abteilung 503*) in the lead, began their breakthrough toward Cherkassy. Shown in the photograph is *Oberstleutant* Franz Bäke, one of the most successful and highly decorated *Panzertruppen* officers.

A sudden thaw on 5-6 February turned the battlefield into a quagmire. The wheeled fuel tankers and ammunition trucks could not move and the *III. Panzer-Korps* was bogged down. The light vehicles, such as this *Kubelwagen*, still had a chance of passing through the mud on the "road". (Fabiger, Feb. 1944)

In the photograph, an *SS* commander is preparing for combined operations by *"LSSAH" Tigers* and *StuG's* as part of the operation to penetrate toward Cherkassy. The obsolete *Pz Bef Wg III Ausf K's* were retained as command vehicles in armored detachments until mid–1944. In the background are *Tiger* tanks. (Adendorf, Feb. 1944)

There was so much mud that the tanks at the front line had to receive fuel in buckets and cans. This photograph best illustrates the difficulties that *"LSSAH"* soldiers faced when trying to pull their vehicles out of the mud with requisitioned agricultural tractors. (Adendorf, Feb. 1944)

While waiting for the command to advance, the *SS-Panzergrenadiere* sat on the ground, partially protected by the *StuG's*, to present a smaller target in the open space. There was always the danger of a bullet or shell flying in from somewhere. (Adendorf, Feb. 1944)

SS-Panzergrenadiere anticipate the order to move out. They may be the intended mounted infantry for the *Tigers* visible in the background. (Adendorf, Mar. 1944)

After receiving orders, the commanders head to their vehicles. In the distance, a *Tiger* with its long-range main gun screens the space for the concentration of *SS-Panzergrenadiere* and assault guns. (Adendorf, Feb. 1944)

It is just possible to see that the rear of the turret on this *Tiger* carries the number "412" on the small plate. This is a mystery, since "*LSSAH*" and "*Totenkopf*" *Tigers* used individual tank numbers, which began with the number 4 (4th company) in the winter of 1942/43. The *Heer* heavy companies had starting numbers no greater than 3. The tank in the background was manufactured after July 1943 and this is certainly a photograph taken in the winter of 1943/44. It is possible that the crew retained the old number and put it back on the tank, particularly since this unit was left with very few operational tanks. (Adendorf, Feb. 1944)

A heavy Russian KV-1B tank (Klementi Voroshilov, named after the Soviet Commissar for Defense). Combat experience resulted in extensive uparmoring to 110 mm on the hull and turret. The KV-1C variant had a basic 90 mm hull armor thickened with an extra 40 mm plate. The extra armor increased the weight to 44 tons and reduced the speed to 30 km/h. Although the German *Tigers* and *Panthers* destroyed the KV tank at distances of up to two kilometers, it was a tough nut to crack for the *PzKpfw IV's* and *StuG III's*. (Adendorf, Feb, 1944)

The crew of the *SS* assault gun looks over the destroyed KV-1B. The officer in the grey uniform and the soldier on the tank are holding their pistols in hand just in case a surviving crewmember is hiding in the vehicle. Maps and other information, that could be useful in revealing the strength and intentions of the enemy, were frequently found in the abandoned tanks. (Adendorf, Feb. 1944)

9.s.SS-Pz.Kompanie "Totenkopf", December 1943

Stab

1.Zug

2.Zug

3.Zug

4.Zug

5.Zug

A group of *"Totenkopf"* soldiers use a Soviet KV-1 as shelter. In September 1942, all of the division's personnel were ordered to adopt the script *"Totenkopf"* cuff title. However, as can be seen in this photograph, some veterans continued to wear the "Death's Head" insignia which was actually *Allgemeine* (General) *SS* insignia. All the crewmen appear to be wearing the one-piece winter coverall that was reversible (greenish grey/white). In some cases it appears to be worn under additional layers of clothing. (Adendorf, Mar. 1944)

The *SS-Panzergrenadiere* and kneeling mortar crew receive orders before commencement of operations. The *kz. 8 cm Gr.W.42 (Stummelwerefer)* was originally intended for use by airborne and special-purpose units. However, gradually, it replaced the small *5 cm le.Gr.W.34* as the standard light infantry mortar. (Ahrens, Feb. 1944)

An *MG 34* machine gun has been positioned in a trench. The white-uniformed *SS* soldiers, and the fresh snow which fell upon the weapons and ammunition boxes, make the position virtually invisible. The special sight and tripod indicate that the *MG 34* is prepared for long-range fire. (Ahrens, Mar. 1944)

Ten 7.92 mm rounds were packed into each cardboard box. Taking out the rounds and putting them into 100-round machine gun belts was no easy task, particularly when the outside temperature was below freezing. There was a mechanical device that belted ammunition but these soldiers obviously do not have one at hand. (Ahrens, Mar. 1944)

A final check is performed before heading out on an operation. Each of the grenadiers carries two metal ammunition boxes, each holding up to 300 rounds. (Rottensteiner, Mar. 1944)

The reversible white/camouflage parka and trousers, model 1943, were manufactured exclusively for *Waffen-SS* troops.

A group of *"LSSAH"* soldiers awaits orders. The soldiers in the photograph are wearing either long, green winter parkas lined with rabbit fur, or short, padded reversible parkas with the green side out and the white side in. The officer wears the 1942 pattern felt boots made of high grade leather.(Adendorf, Feb. 1944)

There were approximately 30 *StuG's* in the Cherkassy Pocket. The *"Wiking"* had approximately 6 in its 4th Company, the *"Wallon" Brigade* had a *StuG* Company, and *StuG Abt. 239* had less than a dozen guns and another 4 in the maintenance facility near Goroditsche. These 4 vehicles, led by Willy Hein from the *"Wiking"*, helped to maintain the southern defensive front around the village of Olshana.

A column of *"Wiking"* infantry marches inside the pocket. Thanks to the poor visibility, the Cossack cavalry succeeded in breaking through these columns in several attacks, partially destroying them.

German soldiers retreat in a disorganized manner from the Cherkassy Pocket. At the end of the retreat, these soldiers faced a river they had to swim across. This photograph was taken by *SS-Kriegsberichter* Jarolin, who also swam across the river. Judging by the photograph, he succeeded in saving the film.

After battling for 32 kilometers, the *"LSSAH"* succeeded in penetrating to the pocket and across the Gniloy Tikich stream, establishing a bridgehead on 8 February. A sudden thaw turned the battlefield into a quagmire and only the tracked vehicles could move without difficulty. The photograph shows *"LSSAH"* troops on the move toward Cherkassy. (Jarolim, Feb. 1944)

The *3. Panzer-Division* also participated in the breakthrough operation. The photograph shows a *PzKpfw IV* of the division moving at full speed. It appears to have just come out of the maintenance facility, where it received new mud guards and turret side skirts. Its crew did not have the time to paint them white. (Kraus, Feb. 1944)

Waiting for the survivors from the Soviet encirclement. (Jarolim, Feb. 1944)

A *"Wiking"* officer wearing a field cap and an NCO in a peaked service cap, were photographed near Cherkassy before the heavy snowfall. In December 1939, the new field cap for officers (*Feldmütze für Führer neuer Art*) was introduced. The cap was designed to be easily folded away so that the soldier could place a helmet on his head. The general practice of adding a branch-of-service color — *Waffenfarbe* in German — had long since been phased out of service by this time, although it continued to be worn on the overseas caps by many soldiers until war's end. In this case, it would appear that the color is infantry white (Jarolin, Mar. 1944)

The troops had overcome the final barrier on their mission to rescue the forces, the Gniloy Tikich, by swimming the stream, for under the strong Soviet pressure, it was not possible to put up a pontoon bridge. The photograph shows a convoy of surviving soldiers who had thrown aside all their unnecessary personal equipment and weapons in order to cross the swollen stream. (Jarolim, Feb. 1944)

TARNOPOL
KAMENETS/PODOLSK
11 - 30 April 1944

In early March 1944, massive Russian breakthrough forces succeeded in encircling 22 divisions of von Manstein's field-army group in a large pocket around the town of Kamenets Podolsk. Among the cut-off forces, were the *"Leibstandarte"* and *"Das Reich"* divisions. Also encircled in the pocket was the heavy tank-destroyer battalion *schwere Panzerjäger-Abteilung 88* with its *Nashorn* tank destroyers, photographed by *SS-Kriegsberichter* Brockhausen.

In the difficult climatic conditions that existed during that winter on the Eastern Front, horse-drawn wagons were frequently the only possible form of transportation, and were equally used by the Germans and Russians. However, a large number of horses were killed in the combat zone. In this photograph, an *SS PzKpfw IV* has entered an occupied area, and the dead horses appear to be from the Russian side. An outlined "601" is recognizable on the tank. (Ahrens, Mar. 1944)

In this photograph taken in the pocket, a *StuG III* of the *"LSSAH"* and a column of *Nashorns* of *schwere Panzerjäger–Abteilung 88* are visible. With the help of the *9. SS-Panzer-Division "Hohenstaufen"* and *10. SS-Panzer-Division "Frundsberg"*, which arrived from France on 6 April, the Soviet encirclement was broken and the German forces succeeded in escaping from the pocket. (Lindekens, Mar. 1944)

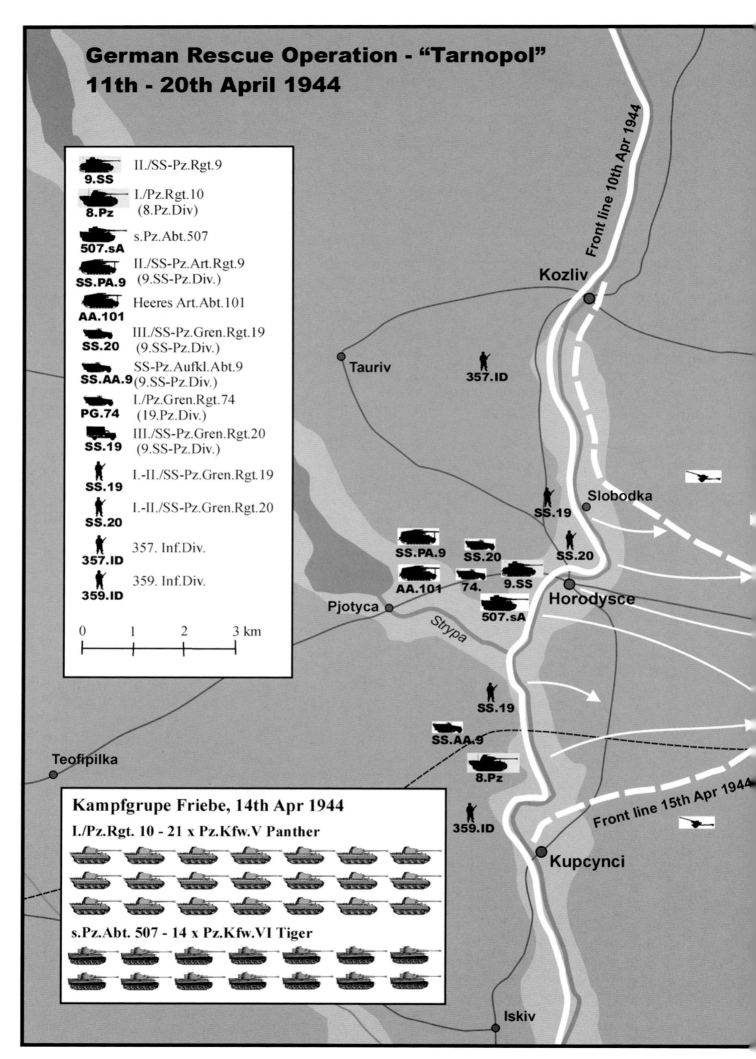

German Rescue Operation - "Tarnopol"
11th - 20th April 1944

Legend:

9.SS	II./SS-Pz.Rgt.9
8.Pz	I./Pz.Rgt.10 (8.Pz.Div)
507.sA	s.Pz.Abt.507
SS.PA.9	II./SS-Pz.Art.Rgt.9 (9.SS-Pz.Div.)
AA.101	Heeres Art.Abt.101
SS.20	III./SS-Pz.Gren.Rgt.19 (9.SS-Pz.Div.)
SS.AA.9	SS-Pz.Aufkl.Abt.9 (9.SS-Pz.Div.)
PG.74	I./Pz.Gren.Rgt.74 (19.Pz.Div.)
SS.19	III./SS-Pz.Gren.Rgt.20 (9.SS-Pz.Div.)
SS.19	I.-II./SS-Pz.Gren.Rgt.19
SS.20	I.-II./SS-Pz.Gren.Rgt.20
357.ID	357. Inf.Div.
359.ID	359. Inf.Div.

0   1   2   3 km

Kozliv

Front line 10th Apr 1944

Tauriv

357.ID

Slobodka

SS.19

SS.PA.9   SS.20   SS.20

AA.101   74.   9.SS

Pjotyca

507.sA

Horodysce

Strypa

SS.19

SS.AA.9

Teofipilka

8.Pz

Front line 15th Apr 1944

359.ID

Kupcynci

Kampfgrupe Friebe, 14th Apr 1944

I./Pz.Rgt. 10 - 21 x Pz.Kfw.V Panther

s.Pz.Abt. 507 - 14 x Pz.Kfw.VI Tiger

Iskiv

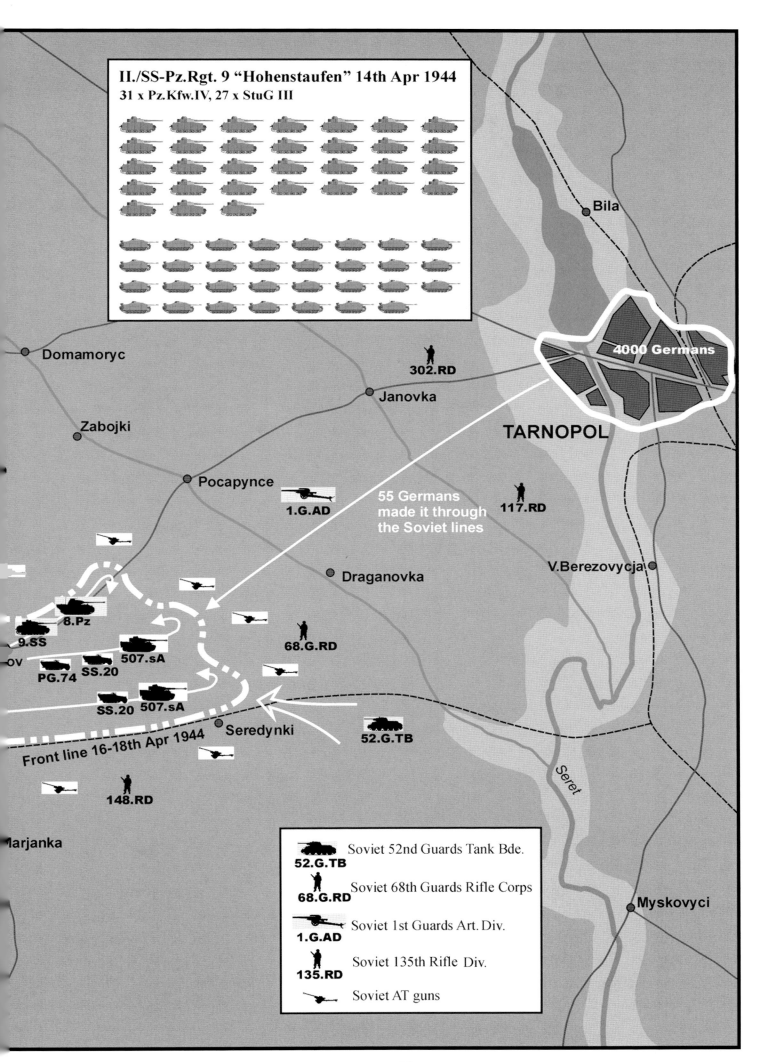

II./SS-Pz.Rgt. 9 "Hohenstaufen" 14th Apr 1944
31 x Pz.Kfw.IV, 27 x StuG III

Bila

Domamoryc

302.RD

Janovka

4000 Germans

Zabojki

TARNOPOL

Pocapynce

55 Germans
made it through
the Soviet lines

1.G.AD

117.RD

V.Berezovycja

Draganovka

8.Pz

9.SS

507.sA

68.G.RD

PG.74   SS.20

SS.20   507.sA

Seredynki

52.G.TB

Front line 16-18th Apr 1944

Seret

148.RD

Marjanka

Myskovyci

	Soviet 52nd Guards Tank Bde.
52.G.TB	
	Soviet 68th Guards Rifle Corps
68.G.RD	
	Soviet 1st Guards Art. Div.
1.G.AD	
	Soviet 135th Rifle Div.
135.RD	
	Soviet AT guns

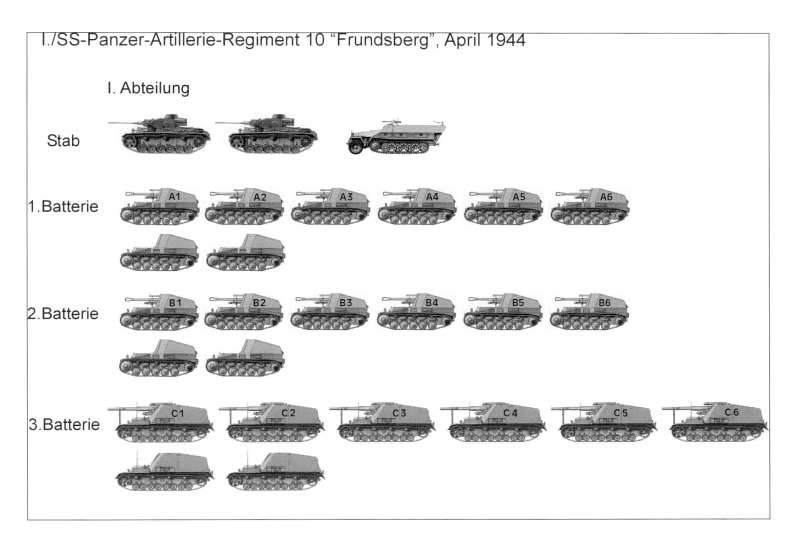

I./SS-Panzer-Artillerie-Regiment 10 "Frundsberg", April 1944

I. Abteilung

Stab

1.Batterie   A1 A2 A3 A4 A5 A6

2.Batterie   B1 B2 B3 B4 B5 B6

3.Batterie   C1 C2 C3 C4 C5 C6

Opposite page top: At the end of December 1943, the *6. SS-Freiwilligen Sturm-Brigade "Langemarck"* was attached to the *"Das Reich"*. They fought together in the pocket. The photograph shows a Flemish *StuG III* from the *Sturm-Brigade* that, together with the *"Das Reich"*, fiercely defended the eastern side of the pocket. (Lindekens, Mar. 1944)

Oppsite page bottom: On 23 March 1944, a *"Langemarck"* commander of a *StuG III*, *SS-Untersturmführer* Heyenck, and his driver, were decorated with the Iron Cross Second Class for their display of courage during the battle in the Kamenets Podolsk Pocket.

In this photograph taken in February 1944, a column of *StuG*'s and completely new *Hummel* self-propelled artillery, fresh from the factory and painted yellow, move across the muddy steppe. The first *StuG III*'s with the so-called *Saukopf* (sow's head) gun mantlet, as seen on the first vehicle in the column, were delivered to the units in January 1944.

The *6. SS-Freiwilligen Sturm-Brigade "Langemarck"*, 2,020 strong, was composed of Flemish and Finnish volunteers organized into two battalions. Part of the brigade's composition was a *StuG* company with 11 vehicles, an antitank company, a light artillery battery, an antiaircraft company, a heavy machine-gun company and three infantry companies, all motorized. The photograph shows a light *2 cm Flak 38* antiaircraft gun, which the Flemish crew used to fire at ground targets.

A destroyed T-34 Model 1943 of the Third Guards Tank Army near the town of Buchach, where the encirclement was broken. After a successful withdrawal of the encircled forces, their commander, *Generaloberst* Hans Hube, reported to the headquarters the destruction of 358 Russian tanks, 190 field artillery pieces, 29 assault guns, 4 self-propelled guns and numerous hand-held weapons.

Two German heavy 18-ton *SdKfz 9* halftracks tow away the spoils of war – a captured, damaged Russian self-propelled gun (probably an SU-122 armed with an M38 field howitzer). Frequently, the Germans, if they did not repair them, used the damaged Russian vehicles as well-armed bunkers.

SS artillerymen fire a heavy *150 mm SiG 33* infantry gun. Such guns belonged to the support companies of the *Panzergrenadier* regiments. Due to their short range of five kilometers, they were only used in close-support fire missions, rather than long-range shelling, for which the guns from the artillery regiment were employed.

After the successful breakthrough toward the pocket, on 11 April the *9. SS-Panzer-Division "Hohenstaufen"* was ordered to rescue 4,000 Germans trapped in Tarnopol. This photograph shows men of the I./SS-Panzer-Grenadier-Regiment 19 anticipating the order to attack. Note the large amount of arms and ammunition they will take with them. (Raudies, Apr. 1944)

Another view of the SS-Panzergrenadiere of the "Hohenstaufen" division. The earthen embankment the soldiers are standing on served well to cover the vehicles that brought in the soldiers and ammunition. (Raudies, Apr. 1944)

German vehicles assemble before the attack on Tarnopol. In the background, it is possible to recognize *SdKfz 250* APC's, two *150 mm SiG.33* infantry guns (along with their *Sd.Kfz.11* prime movers) ready to fire, and a single 75mm antitank gun.

SS-Gruppenführer and Generalleutnant der Waffen-SS Wilhelm Bitrich commander of the *"Hohenstaufen"*, was photographed during the fighting near Tarnopol. The cross and the number "45" on his command *SdKfz 251* are painted on as a white outline. (Raudies, Apr. 1944)

Generalfeldmarschall Walther Model, commander of *Heeresgruppe Nordukraine*, observes near Tarnopol from his personal *SdKfz 251* halftrack. On 28 June 1944, he was given command of the remnants of *Heeresgruppe Mitte*. Model was an extremely capable general whose flair earned him the nickname "The *Führer's* Fireman".

The grenadiers used the Russian antitank ditch as a starting point for the attack. Note the grenadier wearing an ammunition belt over his shoulder and carrying an ammo box that held 300 rounds of 7.92 mm ammunition. (Grönert, Apr. 1944)

In the breakthrough operation toward Tarnopol, the *"Hohenstaufen"* only had one tank battalion, the *II/SS-Panzer-Regiment 9*. Its 5th and 6th companies had *PzKpfw IV* tanks and the 7th and 8th companies had *StuG's*. On 14 April, the *II/SS-Panzer-Regiment 9* had 31 operational *PzKpfw IV's* and 27 *StuG's*. In this photograph, taken near Horodyszcze on 16 April, the *PzKpfw IV* uses the destroyed T–34 tanks as cover. (Raudies, Apr. 1944)

Although 30 *Panthers* and 14 *Tigers* from the *"Panzerverband Friebe"*, and *Tigers* from the *sPzAbt 507* participated in the attack alongside the *9. SS–Panzer–Division "Hohenstaufen"*, the assault was halted only 8 kilometres from Tarnopol. By 17 April, *"Hohenstaufen"* had 18 operational *PzKpfw IV's* and 6 *StuG's*, and its total losses included 13 tanks and 21 assault guns. The enemy lost a total of 74 tanks, 84 guns and 21 antitank guns. (Raudies, Apr. 1944)

The initial attack toward Tarnopol bogged down in the mud, which cost the Germans the element of surprise and gave the Russians an opportunity to strengthen their positions with numerous antitank guns. The most numerous among them were the 76mm ZiS-3 Model 1942 (shown in the photograph) and 57mm Model 1941/43 antitank guns. The ZiS-3 gun was composed of a total of 913 parts and, due to its simple construction, was mass-produced on conveyer belts. At the end of 1942, a single factory produced 120 such guns per day. Due to its low silhouette, a well dug-in and camouflaged antitank gun was very hard to spot on the battlefield. To a tank commander such as Michael Wittmann, a destroyed antitank gun was worth as much as a tank.

Hummeln sit in position near Tarnopol. The snow has melted, making the whitewashed vehicles very visible. For this reason, one of the crew members covered his vehicle with the shelter halves.

SS-Panzerjägerabteilung 9 "Hohenstaufen", 1944

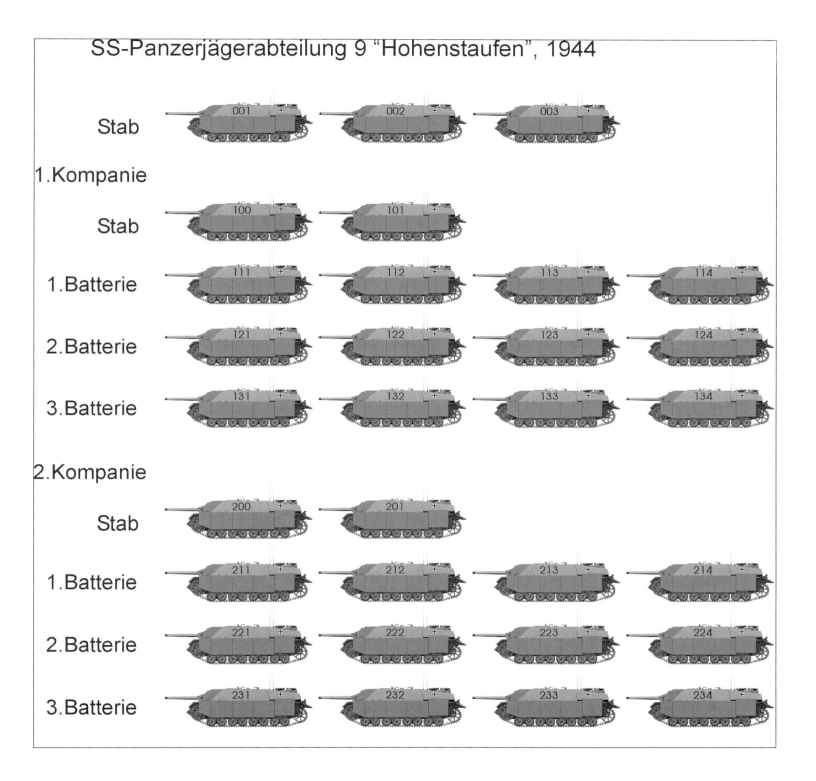

Stab

1.Kompanie

Stab

1.Batterie

2.Batterie

3.Batterie

2.Kompanie

Stab

1.Batterie

2.Batterie

3.Batterie

A *Wespe* from the *"Hohenstaufen"* fires over open sights at ground targets. During an attack, the armored self-propelled howitzers moved several hundred meters behind the tanks. On the rear right side of the *Wespe* superstructure is visible a large letter "E", indicating that this is the 5th battery. (Adendorf, Apr. 1944)

"Hohenstaufen" Panzergrenadiere in an *SdKfz 251* APC before Tarnopol. On the left is an *SS-Hauptsturmführer* (Captain) and right behind him is an *SS-Hauptsharführer* (Sergeant First Class). (Raudies, Apr. 1944)

SS soldiers with a dog during a rest period following the battle at Tarnopol. In the background is an *SdKfz10* halftrack. Its camouflage consists of a dark yellow base, oversprayed with an olive-green pattern. (Raudies, Apr. 1944)

Evacuating wounded under the protection of the APC's. The losses in the division were significant. In three days, 1,383 men were lost. Only 53 of the 4,000 surrounded Germans succeeded in breaking out of Tarnopol through the Russian positions. Note the three different camouflage uniforms on the soldiers carrying the wounded. (Raudies, Apr. 1944)

BREAKTHROUGH TO KOVEL
27 March - April 1944

After the retreat from the Cherkassy Pocket, the *SS-Panzergrenadiere* of the *"Germania"* and *"Westland"* regiments of the *"Wiking"* division were in a sorry state. All of the heavy weapons, and a great portion of personal weapons and equipment, had been lost. Some of this was replaced from German warehouses nearby, and then both regiments were sent by rail to Kovel (Kowel), a key rail and road junction on the Polish-Ukrainian border. The men had just arrived in Kovel on 16 March 1944, when four infantry divisions and a regiment of tanks of the 2nd Byelorussian Front encircled the city. This bleak photograph shows a German soldier on guard duty in Kovel.

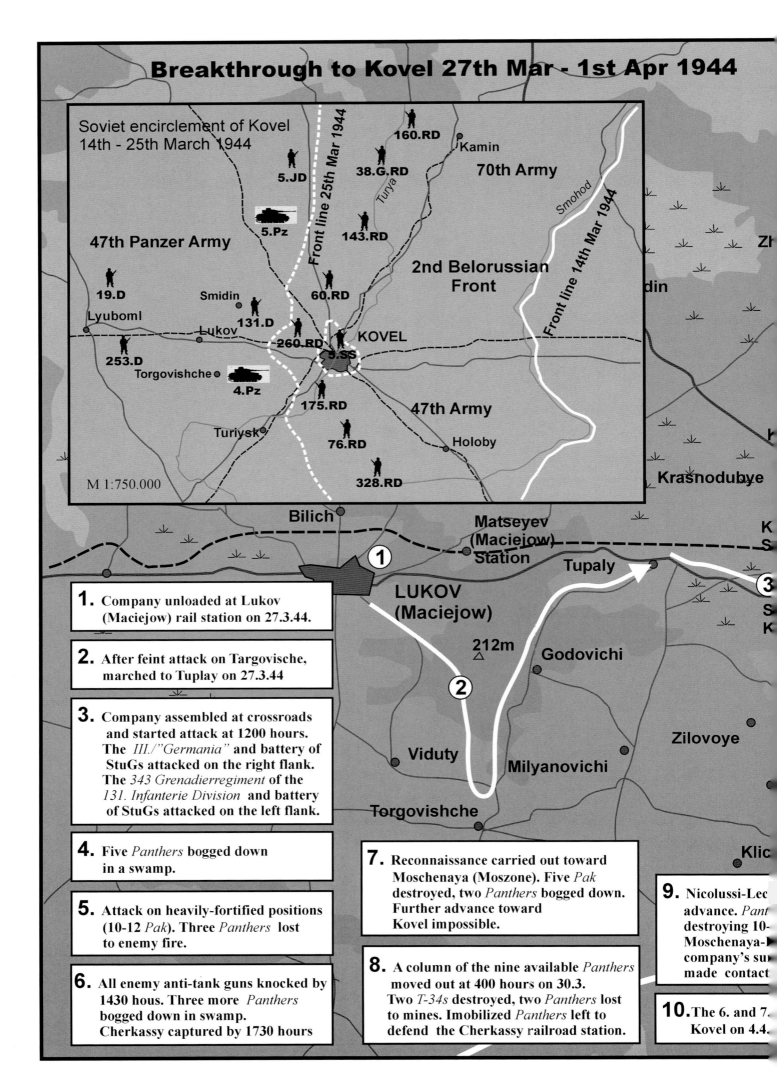

Breakthrough to Kovel 27th Mar - 1st Apr 1944

Soviet encirclement of Kovel 14th - 25th March 1944

Front line 25th Mar 1944

Front line 14th Mar 1944

160.RD

Kamin

38.G.RD

70th Army

5.JD

Turya

Smohod

5.Pz

47th Panzer Army

143.RD

Zh

2nd Belorussian Front

19.D

Smidin

60.RD

Lyuboml

din

131.D

Lukov

260.RD

KOVEL

253.D

5.SS

Torgovishche

4.Pz

175.RD

47th Army

Turiysk

76.RD

Holoby

328.RD

Krasnodubye

M 1:750.000

Bilich

Matseyev
(Maciejow)
Station

K S

Tupaly

① 1

LUKOV
(Maciejow)

③ 3

1. Company unloaded at Lukov (Maciejow) rail station on 27.3.44.

212m △

Godovichi

S K

2. After feint attack on Targovische, marched to Tuplay on 27.3.44

② 2

3. Company assembled at crossroads and started attack at 1200 hours. The *III./"Germania"* and battery of StuGs attacked on the right flank. The *343 Grenadierregiment* of the *131. Infanterie Division* and battery of StuGs attacked on the left flank.

Zilovoye

Viduty

Milyanovichi

Torgovishche

Klic

4. Five *Panthers* bogged down in a swamp.

7. Reconnaissance carried out toward Moschenaya (Moszone). Five *Pak* destroyed, two *Panthers* bogged down. Further advance toward Kovel impossible.

9. Nicolussi-Lec
advance. *Pant*
destroying 10-
Moschenaya-
company's su
made contact

5. Attack on heavily-fortified positions (10-12 *Pak*). Three *Panthers* lost to enemy fire.

6. All enemy anti-tank guns knocked by 1430 hous. Three more *Panthers* bogged down in swamp. Cherkassy captured by 1730 hours

8. A column of the nine available *Panthers* moved out at 400 hours on 30.3. Two *T-34s* destroyed, two *Panthers* lost to mines. Imobilized *Panthers* left to defend the Cherkassy railroad station.

10. The 6. and 7.
Kovel on 4.4.

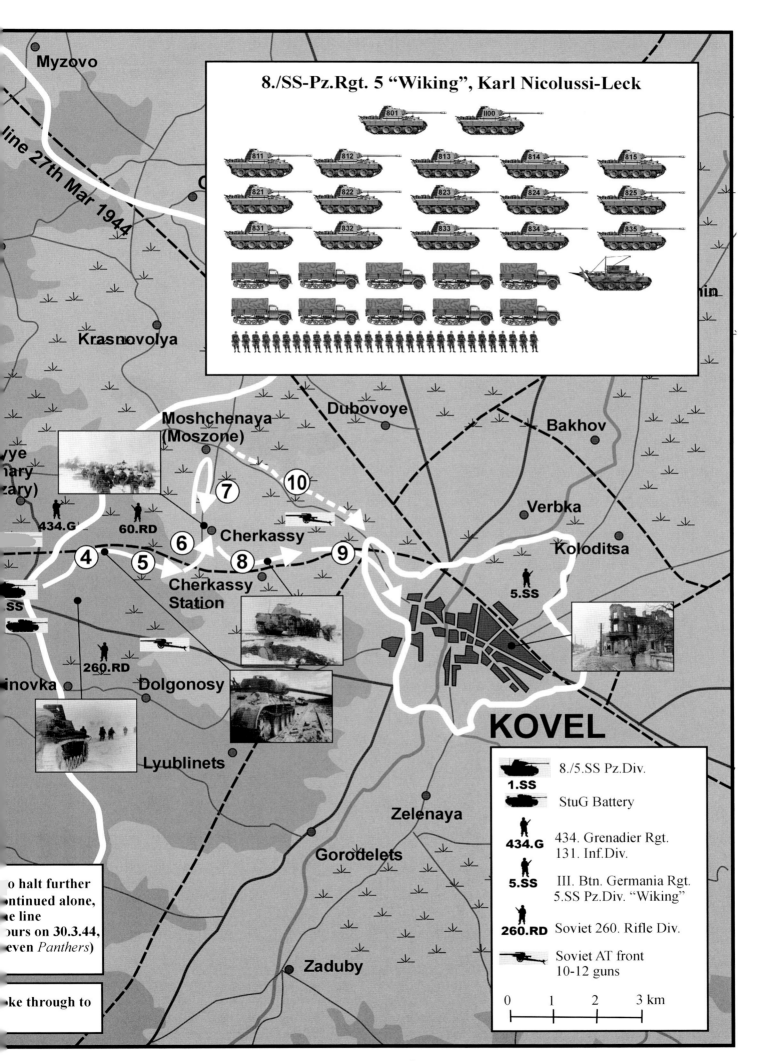

8./SS-Pz.Rgt. 5 "Wiking", Karl Nicolussi-Leck

Myzovo

line 27th Mar 1944

Krasnovolya

Moshchenaya
(Moszone)

Dubovoye

Bakhov

Verbka

⑦

⑩

434.G

60.RD

Cherkassy

Koloditsa

④

⑤

⑥

⑧

⑨

5.SS

Cherkassy
Station

260.RD

Dolgonosy

KOVEL

Lyublinets

Zelenaya

Gorodelets

o halt further

ntinued alone,
e line
urs on 30.3.44,
even *Panthers*)

ke through to

Zaduby

	8./5.SS Pz.Div.
1.SS	
	StuG Battery
434.G	434. Grenadier Rgt. 131. Inf.Div.
5.SS	III. Btn. Germania Rgt. 5.SS Pz.Div. "Wiking"
260.RD	Soviet 260. Rifle Div.
	Soviet AT front 10-12 guns

0   1   2   3 km

The portion of *"Wiking"* that had escaped encirclement, and the *Panther* battalion (with 79 *Panthers*) that had been forming in Germany since December 1943, were sent to break through to Kovel. This photograph shows *"Wiking"* soldiers unloading ammunition and fuel from an armored train.

III./SS-Panzer-Grenadier-Regiment 9 "Germania" avoided encirclement in Kovel. This battalion and a *Heer* assault gun battery were attached to the *131. Infanterie-Division*. The attack on Kovel was halted due to strong resistance and to await the arrival of a *Panther* company. In the photograph, *"Germania" SS-Panzergrenadiere* advance toward Kovel under the protection of *StuG's*. (Kraus, Mar. 1944)

"Germania" grenadiers and *StuG's* of *Heeres–StuG-Brigade 190* advance toward Kovel through a blizzard. The reduced visibility in such a situation benefited the attacker, particularly if he was advancing over open terrain. (Kraus, Mar. 1944)

On 27 March, the *8./SS-Panzer-Regiment 5*, commanded by *SS Obersturmführer* Nicolussi-Leck, unloaded its *Panthers* at the Maciejow railway station, approximately 20 kilometers west of Kovel. The company had 17 *Panthers*, 1 *Bergepanther* and 10 *Maultiere*. In the photograph, a crew prepares its *Panther Ausf. A* for combat. It is transferring fuel into the *Panther* from 200-liter barrels on the Ford 3000 *Maultiere* (Mule) halftrack. The *Panther's* five internal fuel tanks held 730 liters of fuel, of which 130 were considered as reserve. (Slapak, Mar. 1944)

The tank crew are carrying 11.2 kg heavy *Sprenggranate* (HE) for the 75mm *KwK L/70 Panther* gun. The weight of the *Panzergranate* (AP) was 14.3 kg. Three such rounds were held in each wooden ammo box. The vehicle carried 79 rounds of ammunition for the main gun and 4,200 rounds for two 7.92 mm machine-guns. (Slapak, Mar. 1944)

SS-Pz.Rgt. 5 "Wiking", March 1944

Panzer-Regiment Stabskompanie

Nachr.Zug

Aufkl.Zug

II./SS-Pz.Rgt. 5 "Wiking", March 1944

Panzer-Abteilung II. Stabskompanie

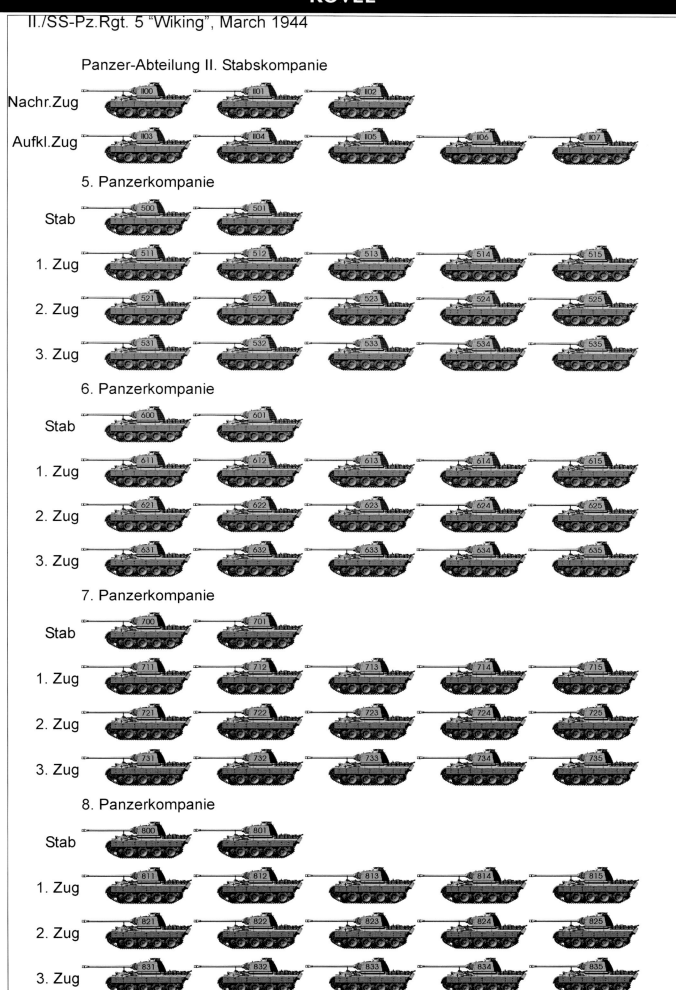

Nachr.Zug

Aufkl.Zug

5. Panzerkompanie

Stab

1. Zug

2. Zug

3. Zug

6. Panzerkompanie

Stab

1. Zug

2. Zug

3. Zug

7. Panzerkompanie

Stab

1. Zug

2. Zug

3. Zug

8. Panzerkompanie

Stab

1. Zug

2. Zug

3. Zug

This *Panther* crewman wears the grey field jacket over the black uniform as further protection from the cold. His *"Dfh.b"* headphones have a leather-covered sprung metal headband, adjustable earpieces and large rubber ear pads that served as both padding and noise insulators. Of interest is the fact that the *Panzer* tunic has had *rosa* (pink) branch-of-service piping applied to both the collar tab and the collar. Although this was not in accordance with regulation, it was a practice increasingly found on *SS* tanker uniforms as the war progressed.(Slapak, Mar. 1944)

A group of officers makes plans prior to a joint action. In the foreground is a *"Germania"* officer in a camouflaged smock, whose pattern is known to collectors as "palm leaf". In the middle is an officer in a grey uniform from the assault gun detachment, while the *"Wiking"* tank officers stand about in their non-regulation private-purchase field caps. Of interest on the cap of the non-commissioned officer is the piping that has been applied to the upturn. It appears to be pink, and, as in the previous photograph, this was a non-regulation addition to the uniform. Bent over the map is (most likely) Nicolussi-Leck. (Slapak, Mar. 1944)

The breakthrough began with the taking of Cherkassy and the ejection of a Soviet infantry battalion. This was a combined effort by *SS* tanks, army assault guns and both *SS* and army infantry. This photograph shows *"Germania" SS-Panzergrenadiere* who, in a great hurry, pass two *Panthers*. The number "825" is visible on the first tank. Following their equipment losses in the Cherkassy Pocket, the grenadiers were dressed in a variety of uniforms from local German warehouses. (Slapak, Mar. 1944)

Only two kilometers from Kovel, the battalion commander ordered Nicolussi-Leck to halt the advance. However, Nicolussi-Leck ignored the radio message and continued the advance with his remaining 9 tanks and accompanying infantry. Several tanks had been disabled by antitank guns and mines. This photograph shows the two wooden beams on the engine deck that became the trademark of the *"Wiking"* tanks. These beams served as a place for grenadiers to sit while catching a ride. (Slapak, Mar. 1944)

"Germania" infantry head toward Kovel in two columns. Since they are not wearing helmets, the enemy is probably not nearby. (Slapak, Mar. 1944)

The terrain on both sides of the railroad embankment was marshy in which the tanks could have bogged down. Without assistance, they could not have been pulled out. Therefore, the elevated embankment offered firm ground to drive on. For this reason, the main driving route was along the railroad lines. *Panther* "834" of *SS–Unterscharführer Melsbach* serves as protection from the wind while the *SS–Panzergrenadiere* dig in. In the background is tank "II00" from the regimental headquarters. It is very likely that Nicolussi-Leck replaced his "800" or "801" with "II00" because of its long-range communication equipment - FuG 7 or 8. (Slapak, Mar. 1944)

Thirty grenadiers from *"Germania"* were volunteers in the breakthrough. The soldier in the photograph is heavily burdened with two boxes of ammunition. On 30 March, Nicolussi-Leck succeeded in penetrating into Kovel and his tanks significantly reinforced the defense of the city. (Slapak, Mar. 1944)

The advance on Kovel could last some time, and so the infantry had to take as much ammunition as they could carry. Note the six additional ammunition pouches on the backpack of the grenadier on the left. (Slapak, Mar. 1944)

The fully-tracked *RSOs* were left in rear, while only one, with the most essential supplies, accompanied the tanks in the advance. However, it too was lost to mines, leaving the tanks and infantry to advance on their own. (Slapak, Mar. 1944)

Nicolussi-Leck and his small group succeeded in penetrating into Kovel. However, the Russians, reinforced with fresh forces of the 175th Rifle Division, again tightened their encirclement. SS-*Panzergrenadiere* from the *III./SS–Panzer–Grenadier–Regiment "Germania"* dig in only several kilometers from the city. (Slapak, Apr. 1944)

A detachment of seven *Heer StuG*'s covers the *"Germania"* positions. Although digging into the sand was relatively quick, the trenches were quite wide. On the other hand, the sandy terrain substantially weakened the effect of the exploding artillery shells. (Slapak, Apr. 1944)

In the open and flat terrain with little vegetation, it was risky to dig into the rare groves of trees because the enemy artillery spotters directed their fire at them. These grenadiers are digging fox holes in the completely open terrain. (Slapak, Apr. 1944)

Without the support of the *StuG*, this infantry position would be untenable. This is actually a *StuG* position, with the infantry as support. A retreat across the open terrain would probably be disastrous. (Slapak, Apr. 1944)

The *Panthers* of 5./*SS-Panzer-Regiment 5* were the last tanks to arrive. The tanks are unloaded at the Maciejow railway station during the first days of April. (Kraus, Apr. 1944)

This brand new *Panther Ausf.A* is completely painted in sand-yellow. A solid coat of white winter paint has been applied to it before it was rail loaded to the Kovel sector. Because the number "511" is in white, for contrast, the area around it has been left without the winter paint. (Kraus, Apr. 1944)

The commander of *SS-Panzer-Regiment 5*, *SS-Obersturmbannführer* Johannes Rudolf Mühlenkamp, in his *PzBe-fWg Panther* "R02" speaks to *SS-Hauptsturmführer* Flügel in *Panther* "800". The headquarters had three command *Panthers*: "R01", "R02" and "R03".

The regimental command post, with Mühlenkamp's "R02". Note, alongside the *Panther*, an obsolete, *kl.Pz.Bef.Wg. I* command vehicle with the insignia of the *3. Panzer-Division* and the word *"Tiger"*. It appears that this vehicle was loaned to the *"Wiking"*. In the background is a *Pionierpanzerwagen SdKfz 251/7* with a small assault bridge and a smaller *SdKfz 250*.

KOVEL

This series of photographs was taken on 4 April, when the second breakthrough toward Kovel was initiated. The *SS-Panzergrenadiere* of the *6.* and *7./SS-Panzer-Grenadier-Regiment "Germania"*, a battery of army assault guns and the *131. Infanterie-Division* participated in the operation. This photograph shows a *Panther Ausf. A* "800" and grenadiers of the *131. Infanterie-Division* advancing toward Kovel.

Panthers of *SS-Hauptsturmführer* Reichert's *6./SS-Panzer-Regiment 5* first succeeded in penetrating into the northern part of Kovel on 5 April. Along the way, they destroyed 10 tanks and 20 antitank guns. During the fighting, the *Panthers* were hit many times, but without suffering substantial damage.

A brand new *SdKfz 251/7 Ausf.D* APC, probably from the SS-*Panzer-Pionier-Bataillon 5*, passes in front of Mühlenkamp's command *Panther* "R02". The vehicle had brackets to carry a small assault bridge, used to cross small obstacles such as trenches.

In the Ukraine, the transition between winter and summer is short. On 30 March, the temperature was -10 degrees C (14 degrees F) and 23 degrees C (74 degrees F) by 16 April. In early April, the sudden warming turned the steppe into a muddy swamp. This photograph shows a *VW Schwimmwagen* of the *"Wiking"* as it drives through the mud. (Jarolim, Apr. 1944)

The amphibious capabilities of the *VW Schwimmwagen* came in handy for driving through pools of muddy water. Note the pointed iron rod on the rear of the vehicle. It was used for finding mines. (Slapak, Apr. 1944)

Covered in mud, an *SS* messenger sits on his motorcycle. This photograph was taken in late February 1944 by *SS-Kriegsberichter* Büchsel, during the short period when snow was replaced by mud.

SS-Gruppenführer Herbert Otto Gille (left), the commander of *"Wiking"*, was likely photographed in Kovel immediately after the penetration of the encirclement. (Jarolim, Apr. 1944)

Destroyed *Panther* "821" on the tracks before Kovel. The tank was knocked out from the flank by Russian antitank guns that were positioned about 600 meters west of Cherkassy. In the action, Nicolussi-Leck lost 15 crewmembers of his company. (Jarolim, Apr. 1944)

A transport convoy advances toward Kovel. At the head of the convoy of *Opel* trucks is an *8-ton SdKfz 7* halftrack, which helped to compact the ground and make the way more easily passable for the remaining vehicles. It was also used to pull vehicles out of the mud.

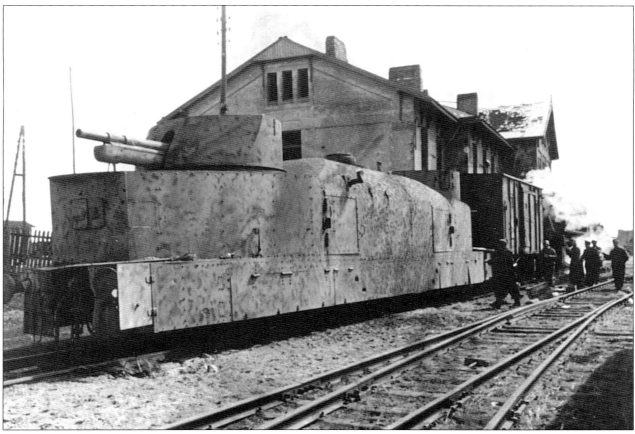

Panzerzug 10, the former Polish "Brave", sits at the Kovel railroad station. In March it fought during the defense of Kovel. At that time, a section of the train was hit by an aircraft bomb. (Jarolim, Apr. 1944)

WARSAW
27 July - 7 August 1944

The tank crews from the *I./SS Panzer-Regiment. 5* that survived the hell at Cherkassy were sent to rest and refit at Cholm, a Polish town near the Ukrainian border. There, on 23 March, the *I. Abteilung* received 22 new *PzKpfw IV's* and, somewhat later, a company of *StuG's*. In April, the *Abteilung* went to train at Heide Training Area at Debica. This photograph shows a column of new *PzKpfw IV Ausf. H's*.

A heavy *Wiking FAMO* 18-ton prime mover at full speed. Three such vehicles were necessary for the recovery of a single disabled *Panther*. The division maintenace battalion had about a dozen *SdKfz 9's*, and three *SdKfz 9/1's* with the 6-ton crane and *SdKfz. 9/2's* with the 10-ton rotary crane.

German armor formations were provided with organic maintenance elements. These companies - *Werkstattkompanien* - were normally assigned at the regiment level. The number of recovery halftracks per company varied, as did the number of trailers. A minimum of three *SdKfz 9 Famo* 18-ton halftracks and two 22-ton *Sd.Anh. 116* flatbed trailers belonged to a company. The trailer was sufficient to transport the 20-ton *PzKpfw IV*, over longer distances. In this photograph, the *Famo* is towing a trailer carrying a *Hummel*.

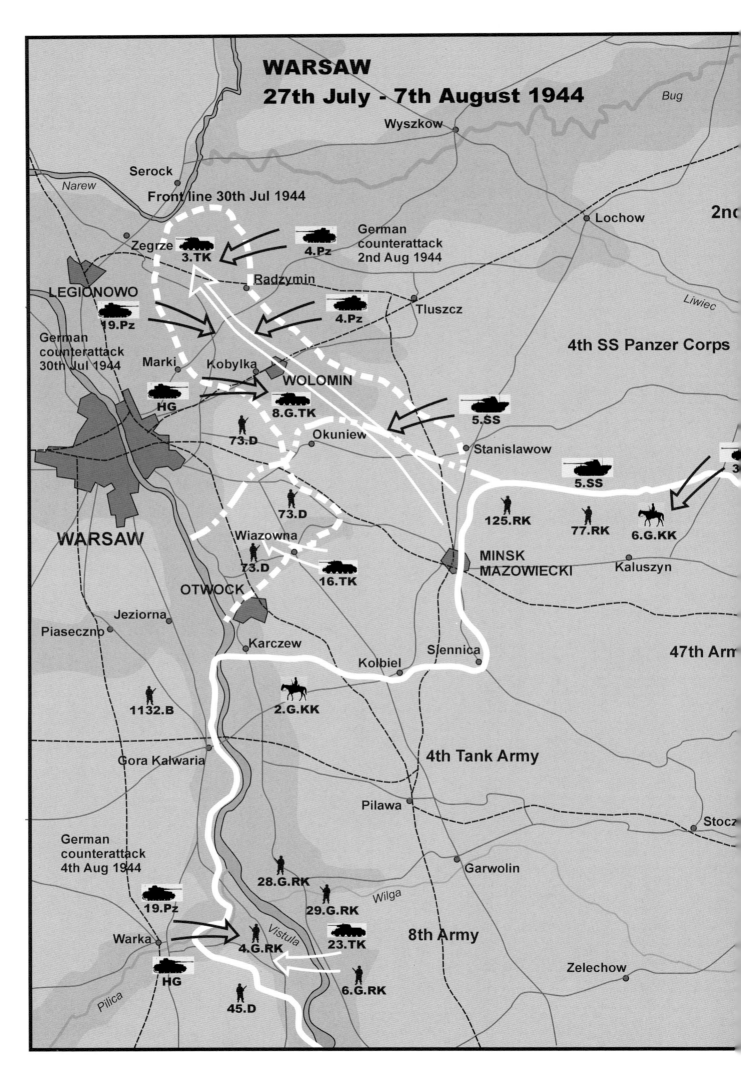

WARSAW
27th July - 7th August 1944

Bug

Wyszkow

Serock

Narew

Lochow

2nd

Front line 30th Jul 1944

Zegrze

3.TK

4.Pz

German
counterattack
2nd Aug 1944

Radzymin

LEGIONOWO

19.Pz

Tluszcz

Liwiec

4.Pz

German
counterattack
30th Jul 1944

Marki

Kobylka

WOLOMIN

4th SS Panzer Corps

HG

8.G.TK

5.SS

73.D

Okuniew

Stanislawow

5.SS

73.D

125.RK

77.RK

6.G.KK

WARSAW

Wiazowna

73.D

MINSK
MAZOWIECKI

Kaluszyn

OTWOCK

16.TK

Jeziorna

Piaseczno

Karczew

Siennica

47th Arm

Kolbiel

4th Tank Army

1132.B

2.G.KK

Gora Kalwaria

Pilawa

Stocz

German
counterattack
4th Aug 1944

Garwolin

28.G.RK

Wilga

19.Pz

29.G.RK

Warka

Vistula

4.G.RK

23.TK

8th Army

Zelechow

HG

6.G.RK

45.D

Pilica

130

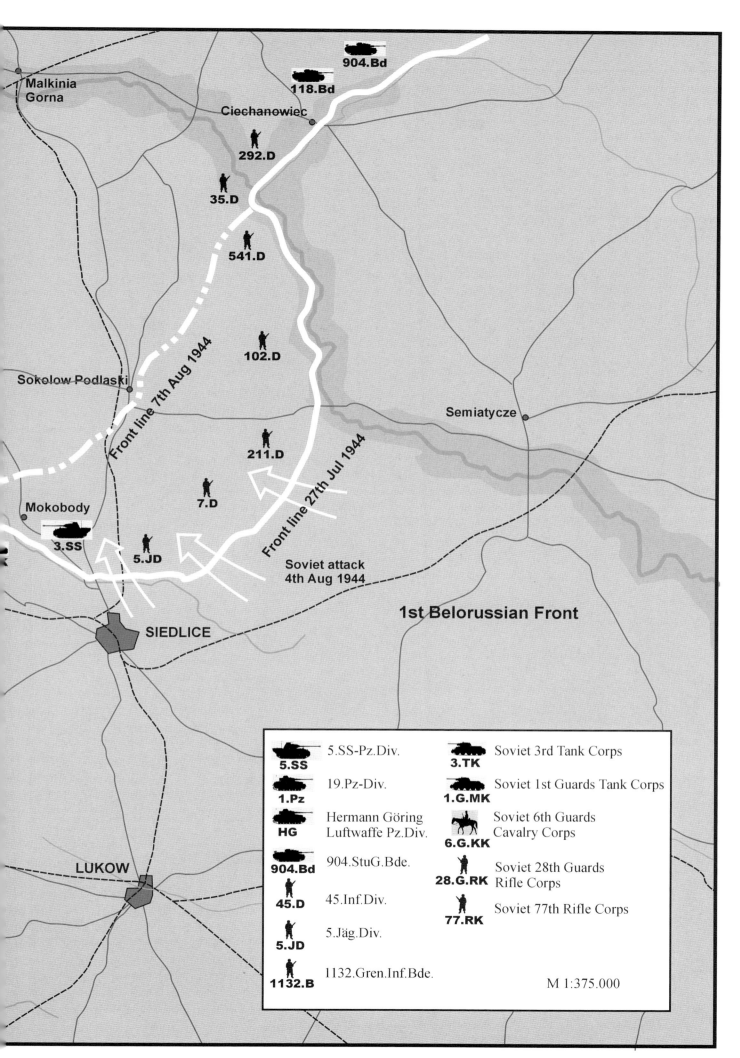

Malkinia
Gorna

904.Bd

118.Bd

Ciechanowiec

292.D

35.D

541.D

Front line 7th Aug 1944

Sokolow Podlaski

102.D

Semiatycze

211.D

Front line 27th Jul 1944

7.D

Mokobody

3.SS

5.JD

Soviet attack
4th Aug 1944

1st Belorussian Front

SIEDLICE

LUKOW

	5.SS-Pz.Div.		Soviet 3rd Tank Corps
5.SS		**3.TK**	
1.Pz	19.Pz-Div.	**1.G.MK**	Soviet 1st Guards Tank Corps
HG	Hermann Göring Luftwaffe Pz.Div.	**6.G.KK**	Soviet 6th Guards Cavalry Corps
904.Bd	904.StuG.Bde.	**28.G.RK**	Soviet 28th Guards Rifle Corps
45.D	45.Inf.Div.	**77.RK**	Soviet 77th Rifle Corps
5.JD	5.Jäg.Div.		
1132.B	1132.Gren.Inf.Bde.		M 1:375.000

In the second battle near Krukel and Maciejow, during 6 and 7 June, the *Panthers* of the *II./Panzer-Regiment 5* knocked out 107 enemy tanks. Note the sprayed camouflage on *Panther* "613".

Note the different camouflage pattern on *Panther* "501" (late *Ausf.D*). This tank belonged to the company commander, *SS-Obersturmführer* Neven du Mont.

The commander of *5./SS-Panzer-Regiment 5*, *SS-Hauptsturmführer* Karl-Heinz Lichte, speaks with his platoon leaders during a commanders' conference. In the background, the commanders of *Panthers* "521" and "522" are carefully observing the horizon.

"Wiking" Panthers between Byalostok and Modlin. In the foreground are the graves of dead crew members. When the Soviets recaptured this area, they removed all traces of the German graves.

Nicolussi-Leck stands in the cupola of his command *Panther* "801". Leaning on the cupola is *SS-Sturmbannführer* Hack, the commander of *"Germania"*. For the successful breakthrough into Kovel, Nicolussi-Leck received the *Ritterkreuz* (Knight's Cross) on 9 April 1944.

The barrel of the *Panther* was a one-piece design and had a removable breech block. During firing, about 70% of the recoil was absorbed by the muzzle brake. The gun could not be fired without the muzzle brake. For many crews, the gun was the best part of the tank. Its *Pzgr 42* antitank round could penetrate 127 mm-thick armor, sloped at 60 degrees, from a distance of 1,500 meters. (Schremmer, May 1944)

During May, *SS–Panzer-Regiment 5* had a period of rest, when it could spend more time on tank maintenance. The divisional maintenance battalion was equipped with a *Strabo* gantry crane (lifting capacity of 16 tons), which was used to lift the tank turrets. (Schremmer, May 1944)

Each *Panzerwerkstattszug* (tank maintenance platoon) had a *15 KN 220/380 V* generator for electric welding. Every day, following a march or combat, something on the tanks had to be welded and repaired. (Schremmer, May 1944)

The final drive was the *Panther's* weakest element. It served as a further reduction of the driving resolution of the engine shaft to the drive sprocket. A large number of abandoned *Panthers* showed evidence of breaks in the final drive. After the war, the French tested captured *Panthers* and estimated that the average final drive life was about 150 kilometers. In the photograph, mechanics repair the final drive. (Schremmer, May 1944)

During May and June 1944, the *"Wiking"* division underwent a battlefield reconstitution. The *SS-Panzergrenadiere* received a large number of medium *SdKfz 251* APC's. The reversed sloped rear plate and the lack of armored cowls on the engine side indicate that this vehicle is an *Ausf. D* variant. (Weiss, May 1944)

In March 1944, all of *Heeresgruppe Süd* fell back to the Dniester River on the border of Romania and was then pushed to the foothills of the Carpathian Mountains. The *"Totenkopf"* dug in at the beginning of May in anticipation of a new Soviet attack. However, May and June were calm, and were used to refit the division. Reinforcements of 6,000 men, new weapons and vehicles arrived. This photograph shows the training of a motorized unit equipped with completely new *VW-Schwimmwagen*. (Göttert, Jun. 1944)

The training vehicles only had the basic equipment and lacked much of the additional equipment required by troops in combat. Note the varying thickness of the tires on the first two vehicles. The lack of raw materials and the large number of manufacturers made vehicle standardization difficult. (Göttert, Jun. 1944)

"Tottenkopf" StuGs and *Schwimmwagen* on the move. It is not clear whether this is part of an exercise or the movement toward Poland. (Göttert, Jun. 1944)

SS-Unterscharführer Felix Przedwojewski, of the *2./SS-Sturmgeschütz–Abteilung 3*, with his *StuG III* and crew. He was awarded the Knight's Cross on 12 December 1943. (Göttert, Jul. 1944)

An *SdKfz 11* halftrack tows a *5.0 cm Pak 38* antitank gun from the *"Totenkopf"*, most probably from the *3./SS-Panzerjäger -Abteilung 3*. Despite the introduction of the more powerful *7.5cm Pak 40* in November 1941, the *Pak 38* continued in service until the end of the war. The company had 12 *Pak 38's/Pak 40's* divided into 3 platoons, each with 4 guns. In the photograph, the crew lies in the grass, waiting for the artillery shelling to end. (Göttert, Jul. 1944)

The full mobilization of German industry resulted in the first significant results in early 1944, when military production was doubled over the preceding year. *Waffen-SS* formations had priority in receiving equipment. This photograph was taken in the Alkett factory in April 1944, and it shows the final phase of *StuG III* production.

SS Sturmbannführer Kaiser from the "*Das Reich*" visits the troops on the Eastern Front. Such visits by veterans and tank experts were part of the propaganda campaign intended to increase troop morale. On his right sleeve, Kaiser wears four tank-destruction strips, each one representing the destruction of an enemy armored vehicle by means of a handheld antitank weapon or device. Note the Knight's Cross around his neck, the German Cross on the right pocket and the Iron Cross on the left pocket of his service tunic. Kaiser was killed in the defense of Nuremberg in 1945 while commanding an *SS-Panzergrenadier* regiment in the *17. SS-Panzer-Grenadier-Division "Götz von Berlichingen"*.

In May 1943, *SS-Panzer-Regiment 3* was ordered to form two additional battalions, each with two *Panther* companies and one *PzKpfw IV* company. However, only the *I./SS-Panzer-Regiment 5* was formed; it had 76 *Panthers* in 4 companies and rejoined the regiment in July 1944.

"Totenkopf" Panthers (Ausf.G) "102" and "111" during a short break. Note the white "Death's Head" insignia near the radio operator's ball mounted *MG 34*. Any external markings on *Panthers*, apart from turret numbers and hull *Balkenkreuz*, were relatively uncommon.

The fighting on the Eastern Front approaches the Polish border. The *II./SS-Panzer-Regiment 5* was transported on 12 July toward Brest-Litovsk, where it met up with the *I./SS-Panzer-Regiment 5* marking the first occasion that the entire regiment was together. This photograph of *Panthers*, most probably from the *7./SS-Panzer-Regiment 5*, was taken during a march across open terrain that offered no possibility of cover from air attacks, although, given the position of the crewmembers, this does not seem of great concern. (Schremmer, Jul. 1944)

In the period between 17 and 20 July, *SS–Panzer–Regiment 5* conducted defensive operations, in which the Russians used a large number of new T-34 tanks armed with 85 mm high velocity guns and heavy JS-I tanks armed with 122 mm guns. This photograph shows destroyed T-34/85's and a JS-I. On 21 July, *SS–Panzer–Regiment 5* had a total of 44 operational *Panthers*, 1 *PzKpfw IV* and 13 *StuG's*. (Schremmer, Jul. 1944)

This photograph was taken during the fighting near the Bug River. It can be assumed that there were no Russian antitank guns in the village about 200 meters in the background, as *Panther* "525" has dangerously exposed its thinly-armored flank. From that distance, even a Russian 45mm antitank gun could destroy the tank.

After the loss of all its *PzKfw IV's*, *I./SS-Panzer-Regiment 5* of the *"Wiking"* was sent back to the Heide Training Area (Debica) to be reconstituted. At the end of July 1944, the first two companies received new *PzKfw IV's*. At the end of August, the *I. Abteilung* was transferred to Lodz in Poland. The two *Abteilungen* of *SS-Panzer-Regiment 5* were together again on 27 August.

The 2. *(gep.)/SS-Panzer-Grenadier-Regiment "Germania"* on the move. In the fighting around Brest-Litovsk, these *SdKfz. 251' APC's* were used for the first time as evidenced by their brand-new appearance. This photograph shows a command *SdKfz. 251/3* on the left and, immediately behind it, two *SdKfz. 251/9's*, armed with the outmoded 75 mm *KwK 37 L/24* guns. Unofficially known as *"Stummel"* (stump), their mission was to provide artillery support. Each of the three *gepanzerte* (mechanized) companies had two such vehicles, while the heavy support company had six.

This photograph was taken in the same place as the preceding one, as evidenced by the tree in the background. Here we see *Panther* "833" and APC "211". (Schremmer, Jul. 1944)

The location of the enemy, or of the area from which an attack could come, can be determined by the direction toward which the gun of *Panther (Ausf. A)* "811" points. The trees provided partial concealment from the air and the ground, although they also tended to limit the ability of the turret to traverse to engage ground targets, particularly when the enemy was at closer ranges. (Schremmer, Jul. 1944)

Two *SS-Panzergrenadiere* stand next to a wheat field in Poland, although it is not easy to spot the one behind the officer. It is difficult to believe that the soldier in the foreground is an *SS-Untersturmführer*, as officers were rarely armed with the *Karabinier K98* rifle. On his belt, he also wears leather rifle ammunition pouches. (Grönert, Jun. 1944)

A reconnaissance patrol moves through a wheat field, in which it was very difficult to find the enemy. Finding fresh tank tracks was an occurrence to be immediately reported to command. (Schremmer, Jul. 1944)

The wheat is as high as this *"Totenkopf" VW-Schwimmwagen*. The crew observes the infantry action nearby. One of them holds a *Panzerfaust* (infantry antitank weapon). (Grönert, Jul. 1944)

Panther "811" is positioned in the open, where its gun could effectively fire up to a distance of 3,000 meters. The smoke in the background shows that this photograph was taken in the vicinity of the fighting. (Schremmer, Jul. 1944)

The 8./SS–Panzer–Regiment 5 and the 2.(gep.) company advance according to all tactical rules. The column of the remaining tanks follows Panther "801" with approximately 100-meter intervals between each vehicle. The Panthers pass by a column of APC's, which are in half-concealed positions. The APC's are also in column, though the spacing between them is greater. (Schremmer, Jul. 1944)

After advancing in column order, the *Panthers* approach the position behind the railway embankment. Behind the embankment, they were protected from enemy fire. (Schremmer, Jul. 1944)

It appears that the embankment position is too exposed for the *Panthers*. They take up a hull-down position behind the railroad tracks instead, from where they still have a clear field-of-fire. (Schremmer, Jul. 1944)

SS-Panzergrenadiere from the 2nd company dug into the embankment, from where they had a good view of the surrounding area. They dug in at intervals of 50 meters, in order to reduce the possible losses from enemy artillery. It appears that the company, which did not have more than 120-130 men, had received the order to occupy a very wide sector. The soldiers' positions had large spacing between them. The soldier in front has just received the Iron Cross, Second Class (it was worn this way on the day of receiving it; thereafter, the ribbon was attached to the tunic). (Schremmer, Jul. 1944)

The smoke in the background could be a burning enemy tank. The recommended operational tactic for the *Panther* was to use the long range of its gun and open fire at large distances. This tactic prevented enemy tanks from approaching to within 1,500 metres because, at that distance, the *Panther* could be destroyed. (Schremmer, Jul. 1944)

A Russian tank crewman surrenders to *Panther* "814". This photograph shows the *Panther's* main external attributes – sloped armor, large road wheels to improve the ride and a long powerful main gun. Note the open ammunition-loading hatch in the turret's rear. (Schremmer, Jul. 1944)

Nicolussi-Leck's *Panther (Ausf. A)* "800" stands next to command *Sd.Kfz. 251/3* "201". Good radio communications were key to the successful application of *Panzer* tactics. The company command vehicles had stronger radios (30 watts instead of 10 watts) and were an important link in the control of *Panzer* formations. As shown in this photograph, nothing could replace face-to-face communications, however. (Schremmer, Jul. 1944)

Note Nicolussi-Leck's "crusher" cap, a type frequently favored by *Panzer* officers. Wearing the head-phones over the top bent the sides and pushed the front back, as is clearly visible in the photograph. Of interest is also the wear of the uniform shorts with the *Panzer* wrap-around tunic. It would seem that any advantage gained to combat the summer heat would have been offset by the wear of the cotton uniform shirt and heavy wool tunic.(Schremmer, Jul. 1944)

Both vehicles, as viewed from the back. Note the star aerial (*Sternantenne "d"*) of the powerful radio set. (Schremmer, Jul. 1944)

The noncommissioned officer on the right wears the *M44* "dot"-pattern camouflage uniform. These were occasionally seen with sleeve eagles and even shoulder straps, but these tended to be on the early production runs of the uniforms. Note the drawn clock on the machine-gun shield, which served to quickly determine the direction of objects around the vehicle. For example, *Panther* "800" is situated at 12 o'clock. (Schremmer, Jul. 1944)

I./SS-Pz.Rgt. 5 "Wiking", July 1944

Panzer-Abteilung I. Stabskompanie

Nachr.Zug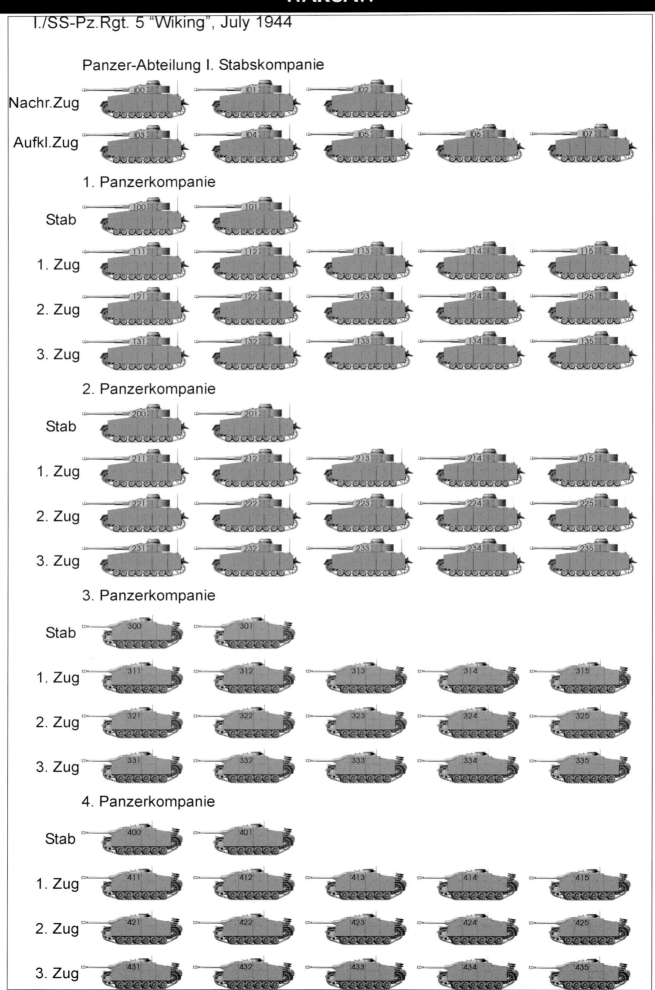

Aufkl.Zug

1. Panzerkompanie

Stab

1. Zug

2. Zug

3. Zug

2. Panzerkompanie

Stab

1. Zug

2. Zug

3. Zug

3. Panzerkompanie

Stab

1. Zug

2. Zug

3. Zug

4. Panzerkompanie

Stab

1. Zug

2. Zug

3. Zug

The same *SdKfz. 251* as featured on page 159 is positioned next to some *Heer* infantry. The authorized strength of an *SS* mechanized-infantry company in 1944 was a headquarters platoon of 3 *SdKfz. 251/3's*, 3 line platoons (each with 3 *SdKfz. 251's*) and a support platoon of 3 *SdKfz. 251/17's*, 2 *SdKfz. 251/2's* and 2 *SdKfz. 251/9's* (Kurbjuhn, Jul. 1944)

A column of *Panthers* moves into the forest. In 1944, the Allied air forces dominated the skies. Among the top priority targets of ground-attack aircraft were German tanks, which were forced to seek concealed positions in wooded areas.

The improved *Panther Ausf. G* came off the factory line in March 1944. The major external difference between the *Panther Ausf. G*, and the earlier *Ausf. D* and *Ausf. A*, was the re-designed hull. The driver's vision port was removed from the front plate to increase strength. The driver's outside vision was provided by a rotating periscope, and his seat could be raised and controls extended so that he could drive with his head out of the hatch, as seen in this photograph.

The *Flak-Abteilung* of a *Panzer-Division* is on the move. At full strength, each of the three heavy batteries in the battalion had six *88mm Flak 37* antiaircraft guns, each pulled by an *8-ton SdKfz 7* semi-tracked tractor (as seen in this photograph), and four *5-ton SdKfz 6/2's*, or *8-ton SdKfz 7/2's*, with mounted *37mm Flak 36* guns. Additionally, the battery was authorized to have *9 VW* staff cars, 2 *Kettenkrader*, 3 *Maultiere*, 6 open cargo trucks and one truck with a box body (also visible in this photograph).

One battery in the *SS-Flak-Abteilung 5* had 12 self-propelled *37mm Flak 36* guns, as seen in this photograph. The *Flak 36* had a practical rate of fire of 80 rpm and had a vertical range of 4,000 meters. The HQ battery had four towed 37mm guns.

An *SS-Hauptsturmführer*, wearing a peaked cap, briefs his platoon leaders. On the cuff title of the man on the right, it is possible to read *"Wiking"*. (Slapak, Jun. 1944)

This APC is covered with camouflage netting, similar to current modern armored vehicles. This practice was rarely seen on the Russian battlefield. It appears that this is a special-purpose staff vehicle that needed to be well hidden. (Schremmer, Jul. 1944)

The *SdKfz 251* APC was intended to transport a mechanized infantry squad of eight soldiers into battle. The vehicle had a well-designed and shaped armored body and a set of wide-opening, double doors at the rear to facilitate a quick exit. The basic variant was armed with two machine-guns.

A wooden bridge across the creek was reinforced with wooden planks so that the 45-ton *Panther* could cross. The ball-mounted hull machine-gun and the driver's hatch are characteristic of the *Ausf.A* version. Note the *Sonnerad* (Sun wheel) *"Wiking"* insignia just behind the headlight. (Schremmer, Jul. 1944)

Captured enemy antitank-gun positions. Under the protection of the *Panthers* of *7./SS-Panzer-Regiment 5*, the *"Wiking" Panzergrenadiere* evacuate their wounded. In the foreground is a destroyed Soviet 76 mm antitank gun. (Kurbjuhn, Jul. 1944)

Covered by *Panther* "724", the *SS-Panzergrenadiere* dig into completely open terrain. Without tanks, the survival of infantry would be impossible in such open terrain. (Kurbjuhn, Jul. 1944)

This *"Totenkopf"* soldier, holding a machine-gun ammunition belt with 100 x 7.92 mm rounds, was probably photographed in a *VW-Schwimmwagen*. He wears the *M44* dot-pattern camouflage uniform, which is also referred to as the "pea" pattern. Early versions of this uniform had provisions for shoulder straps and a factory-applied sleeve eagle; later on, regulations required that no insignia was added, although this edict was often breached. (Schremmer, Jun. 1944)

During the maneuvers held in 1937, the soldiers of the SS-*Standarte "Deutschland"* tested several models of camouflage uniforms. After the manoeuvres, it was estimated that the camouflage uniforms would reduce casualties by 15 percent, which was a sufficient reason to go ahead with their production. By the summer of 1940, the combat units of the *Waffen-SS* had received 33,000 camouflaged smocks and, according to some estimates, a total of almost half a million had been produced by the end of the war. The photograph shows three *SS* soldiers fully dressed in camouflage uniforms.

A group of tired SS-*Panzergrenadiere* and lightly wounded soldiers ride on a *PzKpfw IV*. It appears that they are returning from battle. Note how the tank headlight has been covered with a piece of cloth. (Büschel, Jun, 1944)

Heavily-laden *"Totenkopf"* grenadiers march along a road. Although *SS-Panzer-Divisionen* were fully motorized, often, when the enemy was near, their infantry had to reach their positions on foot. (Schremmer, Jun. 1944)

A battery of camouflaged *Hummel* self-propelled artillery in firing position. Note the few empty casings next to the closest vehicle. Each vehicle could carry 18 rounds, which was sufficient for a short firing mission. Each battery of 6 *Hummels* had two tracked ammunition carriers that carried additional rounds. (Schremmer, Jul. 1944)

A self-propelled *15 cm/sIG33/ auf Sfl 38(t) Ausf.K* heavy infantry gun. It was issued to the infantry gun companies of the mechanized infantry regiments and was used to provide a mobile, direct fire heavy-support weapon. The vehicle quickly acquired the name *Bison*. This company had 3 sections, each with two *Bison* self-propelled guns. The *"Leibstandarte"*, *"Das Reich"*, *"Totenkopf"* and *"Wiking"* also had this type of vehicle.

The *Hummeln*, produced since early 1944, had a crew compartment for the driver and radio operator across the full width of the hull, as seen in this photograph. The crew was made up of six men. The soldiers of the *Panzerartillerie* tended to wear the field-gray version of the *Panzer* uniform, while the tank crews had black uniforms, like the one the "guest" standing on the front end of the vehicle is wearing.

A *Hummel* in firing position. The soldiers carrying the shells and placing them in the vehicle had to be strong, as each one weighed 43.5 kilograms.

The division *Panzerartillerie-Regiment* fielded a formidable array of ordnance. At best, only one or two batteries could be equipped with *Hummeln*. The regiment also had a total of 12 towed *150 mm sFH 18* heavy howitzers and 24 towed *105mm lFH 18* light howitzers.

A well-camouflaged *7.5 cm Pak 40* antitank gun was one of the most formidable weapons that Allied tank crews had to face. This photograph shows the *"Totenkopf" Pak 40* crew that destroyed a T-34 at a distance of about 200 meters. The antitank battalion of an *SS-Panzer-Division* had one or two companies with 12 *Pak 40* guns. The divisional mechanized infantry and reconnaissance units also had strong integral antitank detachments of *Pak 40* guns. (Fabiger, Aug. 1944)

SS-Gruppenführer and *Generalleutenant der Waffen-SS* and commander of the *5. SS-Panzer-Division "Wiking"*, Herbert Gille (left), and *SS-Oberführer* Becher were photographed during conversation in July. At the end of the month, Gille was appointed as commanding general of the new *IV. SS-Panzer-Korps* to lead the *"Wiking"* and *"Totenkopf"*. Note Gille's award of the Diamonds and Swords to the Oakleaves of the Knight's Cross to the Iron Cross, which he received from Hitler for his successful conduct of the battle around Kovel. He was one of only 27 individuals to receive this high distinction. (Schremmer, Jul. 1944)

SS-Oberführer (Brigadier-General) Johannes-Rudolf Mühlenkamp was the commander of *SS-Panzer-Abteilung 5* of the *"Wiking"* division from July 1942. He was decorated with the Knight's Cross for the operation in taking Rostov. In August 1944, Mühlenkamp took over command of the *"Wiking"* from Herbert Gille. Mühlenkamp later became the Inspector General of the Armored Forces of the *Waffen-SS* and survived the war.

On 22 June 1944, the Soviets launched the greatest offensive to date against *Heeresgruppe Mitte* – Operation Bagration. More than 2.5 million soldiers and 5,200 tanks participated in this offensive. A total of 28 German divisions and about 350,000 men were lost. A third of the Eastern Front ceased to exist, and Russian tanks reached the Polish border. In this situation, on 25 June, *"Totenkopf"* was ordered to hold the city of Grodno in order to slow the Soviet advance. Though the strength of the enemy was almost tenfold, the *3.SS-Panzer-Division "Totenkopf"* held the line for 11 days before Model permitted it to withdraw toward Warsaw. This *Pz.Bef.Wg. Panther (Ausf.G) "I02"*, was probably photographed in Grodno or Siedlce, Poland. Note how an enemy round failed to penetrate the 110 mm thick mantlet.

A group of "*Totenkopf*" grenadiers cautiously advances across terrain, in which they had to overcome various obstacles. One soldier has a *Panzerfaust* in case they come across an enemy tank. (Grönert, Aug. 1944)

Two *Kameraden* assist in evacuating a wounded soldier from battle. The possibility of a "*Totenkopf*" soldier surviving imprisonment was virtually zero. The Soviets knew that the division was partially filled with staff from the concentration camps, and therefore they mercilessly settled accounts with each of its wounded or imprisoned soldiers. Knowing what would happen if they fell into Russian hands, the division's troops fought virtually to the very end of human endurance. The fighting between the Soviets and the "*Totenkopf*" was one of the most brutal on the Eastern Front.

After covering almost 700 kilometers in one month, the Soviet forces were exhausted and at the end of their supply line. Model took advantage of this, and, in local counterattacks, succeeded in fending off the Soviet forces advancing toward Warsaw. This also significantly improved the German position. Several Soviet formations were destroyed in these counterattacks. This interesting photograph shows *PzKpfw IV* "II03" from the headquarters of the *II./SS-Panzer-Regiment 3* towing three captured Russian M1942 45 mm antitank guns. They were welcome booty for reinforcing the defense on the Vistula River.

Following the withdrawal from Grodno, the *"Totenkopf"*, and the *Fallshirm-Panzer-Division "Hermann Göring"* held the city of Siedlice for four days against the Soviet 2nd Tank Army. That action permitted the German *2. Armee* to withdraw to the Vistula River. The offensive was halted in early August on the banks of the river. The approach of the Red Army encouraged the Polish Home Army to rise up in occupied Warsaw. The uprising was brutally smothered by *Waffen-SS* formations. The *"Totenkopf"* did not participate. This photograph shows an *SS StuG III* during the fighting in Warsaw.

Taking advantage of the lull, Model reorganized the German defense. He positioned the *IV. SS-Panzer-Korps* (the *"Totenkopf"* and the recently arrived *"Wiking"*) northeast of Warsaw. This photograph shows *"Totenkopf" Panzergrenadiere* with a captured 76 mm antitank gun, on which they have mounted a machine-gun.

Due to the crisis in Poland, *Fallschirm-Panzer-Division "Hermann Göring"* was transferred from Italy. Together with the *"Totenkopf"*, the *"Wiking"*, the *4. Panzer-Division* and the *19. Panzer-Division*, it made up the pillar of Model's defense. This photograph shows a *Marder II* of the division, photographed near Warsaw.

Motorized infantry of the *"Totenkopf"* are on the move somewhere in Poland. Note that the *VW-Schwimmwagens* are armed with *MG42* machineguns, and how small the front license plates are. It appears that the two front vehicles are being towed.

This photograph of the *Panthers* of the Headquarters (Company) of the *I./SS-Panzer-Regiment 3* was taken during the lull. In the headquarters of *I. Abteilung*, there were five *Panthers* in that battalion headquarters. They were numbered "I00", "I01", "I02", "I03" and "I04". The markings of the headquarters *PzKpfw IV's* in the *II./SS-Panzer-Regiment 3* were analogous, e.g. "II00", "II01", etc. (Grönert, Aug. 1944)

This well-camouflaged *Panther* is barely recognizable. The Germans skilfully used camouflage in order to hide from enemy aerial reconnaissance. This masked *Panther* could destroy several enemy tanks before giving away its position. (Grönert, Aug. 1944)

A column of armored vehicles and *VW-Schwimmwagen*, from the *SS-Panzer-Aufklarungs-Abteilung 3* is on the move. The battalion included a company of 30 armored cars. The first two vehicles are *Panzerspähwagen SdKfz 222's*, each armed with an automatic *2 cm KwK30* cannon and an *MG34* machinegun. (Grönert, Aug. 1944)

A *VW-Schwimmwagen* from the reconnaissance battalion, armed with an *MG34* machinegun. The insignia of the division — a *Totenkopf* or "Death's Head" — is partially covered by the entrenching tool. In the background is a *schwere Panzerspähwagen SdKfz 233*. (Grönert, Aug. 1944)

The *SdKfz 233*, armed with the *7.5 cm StuK37 L/24* cannon, was designed to give the armored reconnaissance units a weapon capable of engaging enemy armor and ground targets. It was issued in platoons, each with six vehicles. It was popular with the reconnaissance troops. (Grönert, Aug. 1944)

A *Heer* soldier passes an *SdKfz 233* armored car parked next to the wall of a house. Such positioning made it less visible from the air.

A group of *"Totenkopf"* SS-Panzergrenadiere prepares to move by truck. Only a small portion of the mechanized infantry rode in APC's, the majority used trucks. (Unger, Sep. 1944)

SS personnel have linked up with army tankers, prompting a warm reception on behalf of the personnel of both formations. (Unger, Sep. 1944)

In this photograph, taken by *SS-Kriegsberichter* Grönert near Warsaw in September 1944, it is not clear which unit the *Panther* belonged to. Based on the uniform of the soldier on the right, this is an army tank unit. Most of the tankers appear to be wearing some form of the reed-green herringbone twill *Panzer* uniform, which was worn in summer months because of its lighter weight and its color, which helped armored personnel blend in more with their surroundings once dismounted. Note the poor quality of the equipment belonging to the captured Russian soldier.

These *"Totenkopf"* grenadiers advance along a road. The sandy terrain is characteristic for the region around the Vistula River. (Unger, Sept. 1944)

Judging by the fact that they are carrying only small arms, these *"Totenkopf"* soldiers photographed in a Polish village appear to be a patrol. (Unger, Sept. 1944)

An *SS* grenadier digs a position for a machine-gun nest. Judging by the reserve barrel container on his back, he is the loader in the machine-gun crew. (Unger, Sept. 1944)

Dug-in *"Wiking"* grenadiers observe from their trenches near Warsaw. A *Heer* soldier is in the trench, to the right of the *MG42* crew. (Könnecke, Sep. 1944)

A *"Wiking"* patrol in a Polish village. The patrol leader prepares a written report to be sent by a messenger to the headquarters. (Könnecke, Sep. 1944)

The main Soviet battle tank in the summer of 1944 was the much-improved T-34 armed with an M43 85 mm gun. With the conventional armor-piercing round, it could penetrate armor up to 95 mm thick at a 60 degree angle from a distance of 1,000 meters. This was sufficient to deal with both the *Tiger* and *Panther*. The addition of an extra crewman greatly increased the tank's combat efficiency. The *"Totenkopf"* soldiers look over an abandoned T-34/85. The red star on the turret and glacis plate indicates that this tank was from a Guards Regiment.

German soldiers prized the T-34/85, immediately putting each captured tank to use. To avoid friendly fire, "210" has been clearly marked with large red crosses.

A destroyed Soviet T-34/85 behind two officers of the *"Totenkopf"*. Wearing the black *Panzer* uniform is *SS-Sturmbannführer* Erwin Meierdress, who was commander of the *SS-Sturmgeschutz-Abteilung 3* before becoming commander of the division's armor regiment. Meierdress was a recipient of the Knight's Cross.

SS Tigers were rare in Poland. In early June, the *"Totenkopf"* received 6 Tigers from *schwere SS–Panzer–Abteilung 103*, bringing its total to 15 when it went to Poland. Two *Tigers* were lost at Grodno, but five more were delivered in late July for a total of 18. The *"Wiking"* did not have *Tigers*.

When the Soviets approached Warsaw, the Polish resistance struck at the Germans on 1 August 1944. The armored divisions did not participate in suppressing the uprising, fighting off powerful attacks by Soviet tanks around the city instead. Only the *Tigers* of the *"Totenkopf"* participated in the fighting against the Poles. The Germans lost two *Tigers*, and a number of vehicles were seriously damaged.

Totenkopf" Tiger 912 was photographed near Warsaw in the summer of 1944 during a trial drive following substantial repairs. This *Tiger* is a final production version with a new commander's cupola and all-steel wheels. The vehicle has been completely coated with *Zimmerit*.

A captured American M4 Sherman medium tank. The Americans produced 45,000 Shermans, twice Germany's production of all types of tank. The United States became the tank arsenal of the Allies and large numbers of M4 tanks were supplied to Russia. This photograph shows *"Totenkopf"* tank crewmen riding on a captured Soviet Sherman.

In early August, the *"Wiking"* was transferred by rail east of Warsaw to the area around Modlin, where it was to join *"Totenkopf"*. In this photograph is a column of tanks led by a new *"Wiking" Panther Ausf. G* on the move toward the Vistula River.

"Wiking" Panther "621" in battle around Wieliszew, near Warsaw. On 9 September 1944, *SS-Panzer-Regiment 5* celebrated the destruction of its 500th enemy tank. On the following day, the Soviets began a great new offensive. However, after difficult fighting that lasted two days, they were completely halted. (Jarolim, Sep. 1944)

An *SS StuG* in action. According to a summary by the Chief of Staff of the Army of claimed tank kills on the Eastern Front in the first half of 1944, approximately one third of the enemy tanks were destroyed by tanks, one third by self-propelled guns and one third by antitank guns.

An interesting photograph of *SS StuG's* in Poland, in the summer of 1944. Starting from that time, individual *StuG* crews strengthened the armor of their vehicles with reinforced concrete.

This *"Totenkopf"* *StuG* moves at full speed near Warsaw, raising a great cloud of dust. This kind of driving was dangerous as it could attract the attention of enemy aircraft. (Unger, Sept. 1944)

Another photograph of a *"Totenkopf"* StuG. Note the *Zimmerit* coating and the mounting brackets for the already-lost *Schürzen*. (Unger, Sept. 1944)

Moving through a dense forest, in which there could be lurking enemy soldiers, was a great tactical disadvantage for armored vehicles, as can be seen in this photograph. In close combat, a group of *SS* soldiers captured a column of Soviet SU-85 assault guns.

Totenkopf" SS-Panzergrenadiere near Warsaw. Note the second soldier from the left, who has two belts. (Grönert, Oct. 1944)

The same group of *SS-Panzergrenadiere* passes a *Panther Ausf.A*. (Grönert, Oct. 1944)

A group of *Waffen-SS* officers and soldiers observes the action in the distance. It appears that they are not in direct danger, as, otherwise, they would not be standing so casually. Although different uniforms were produced exclusively for the *Waffen-SS*, the protective coats worn by some of the officers were universal for the entire army.

The *Panther* on the next page photographed from the rear. The right-hand stowage box is also new and lacks the *Zimmerit* anti-magnetic coating, which served as protection against hollow charges. Note the attached snow cleats on the tracks. (Grönert, Oct. 1944)

Panzerkampfwagen IV "521" probably is from the *"Totenkopf"*. This tank has lost its side skirts and back mudguards.

Panther (Ausf. A) "521" of the *"Wiking"* near Warsaw. The new bogie wheels and side skirt show that this vehicle is fresh out of the workshop. The solid rubber tires were not vulcanized to the wheels and could be changed without using any special tools. (Grönert, Oct. 1944)

The Klementi Voroshilov (KV) received significant improvements in mid 1943 with the introduction of a new cast/welded turret, with a frontal armor of 110mm that was fitted to the modified hull of a KV-1. The new turret mounted the new 85mm (M43) gun, resulting in the KV-85. Further developments led to the JS (IS) 1 and 2 which mounted the 122mm gun. The JS-2, introduced in Spring 1944, could hold its own against any German heavy tank. This photograph shows an abandoned JS-2, possibly built by UZTM, that was probably destroyed by its own crew (damage to the main gun barrel).

A destroyed Soviet ISU-122 heavy self-propelled antitank gun. The first vehicles armed with the powerful 122mm A-19S gun appeared in 1944. The design of the ISU-122 was based on the heavy Josef Stalin tank chassis. The gun was mounted in a heavy, 200 mm thick mantlet. Note how the German round penetrated through the weak armor of the crew compartment, where it caused an internal explosion of the ammunition.

The *Bussing-NAG 8-ton SdKfz 7* was used as the mount for the self-propelled *2 cm Flakvierling 38* antiaircraft gun. The vehicle had an armored cab, and its rear superstructure had folding sides to give room for all-round traverse. The divisional *Flak* battalion had 18 such vehicles.

To engage German armor, the Soviets increasingly used partially armored IL-2 ground-attack aircraft. To combat this very dangerous opponent, the anti-air defense of the German armored units was strengthened with the powerful *37mm Flak 36* gun, which could bring down the IL-2 at greater ranges. This 37mm gun mounted on an *SdKfz 7* is being fired at ground targets. (Rottensteiner, Nov. 1944)

At the end of October, the Soviet offensive against Warsaw lost momentum and, following the failure to take Modlin, a short lull ensued. This photograph shows a destroyed Soviet JS-2 tank. (Rührmund, Oct. 1944)

By mid-summer 1944, the *StuG III* assault guns had destroyed about 7,000 Allied tanks. The Soviets issued a special bulletin to their tank crews with instructions for engaging German assault guns. Instead of direct attacks on *StuG* positions, it was recommended that the Soviet tanks by-pass them and attack from the flank or behind. In this photograph taken in Poland, a *StuG* crosses a ditch with the help of a crew member. Note the two armored engine deck cowlings used as extra protection on the front glacis.

This *StuG III Ausf. G* is well set up in its defensive position, from which it could cover with fire the tops of the hills several hundred meters away. In an attack from that direction, enemy tanks would come into German firing range one by one. They would be less able to take advantage of their superior numbers and of firing from greater ranges.

Another view of the same *StuG III*. In the background is a forest into which the *StuG* could rapidly retreat, and where the vehicle could also take up a well-hidden ambush position. The relative lull at the front enabled the crew to dig out a bunker, which served as a shelter from the elements and enemy artillery. (Truöl, Oct. 1944)

The primary purpose of the *StuG's* was infantry support in defense and attack. The presence of the *StuG's* significantly improved the morale of the German infantry, who felt safer in their vicinity. In the armored divisions, the *StuG's* in theory were supposed to have secured the flanks of the tanks in attack and be a mobile reserve in defense. In practice, they were used as tanks and due to their tactical limitations - primarily lack of a fully rotating turret - suffered significant losses. (Truöl, Oct. 1944)

According to the records, in August 1944 the German army had 786 *StuG's*, which in that month destroyed a total of 847 enemy tanks against a loss of 96 of their own. In that month, 312 new *StuG's* were produced, so that the situation still favored the Germans.

SS StuG's stopped on the road. The crews are taking the opportunity for a short rest while the commanders discuss a further course of action.

An *SS StuG* battalion parades in Slovakia. Outdated *StuG's* with short guns were used as command vehicles.

Due to the insufficient production of tanks, and their losses during and after the battle near Kursk, an interim solution for the tank battalions in the *Heer* and the *Waffen-SS* was to fill them with *StuG's*. For the *I./SS-Panzer-Regiment 5 "Wiking"* in January 1944, two companies were planned, each with 22 *StuG's*. Due to the set back at Cherkassy, the delivery was delayed until May 1944. It is not possible to determine exactly how many *StuG's* reached the *"Wiking"*. In January, *"Hohenstaufen"* and *"Frundsberg"* each received two companies of 22 *StuG's*; *II./SS-Panzer-Regiment 9* and *II./SS-Panzer-Regiment 10*. In November 1944, two companies of 14 *StuG's* each were delivered to *II./SS-Panzer-Regiment 3* of the *"Totenkopf"*. This photograph shows a column of *StuG's* somewhere on the northern front. Of interest are the huge crew-stowage boxes that have been added to the rear deck of both assault guns.

The lull at the front meant intensive scouting and a need for accurate assessment of the strength and intentions of the enemy. Aggressive and risky scouting increased the possibility for collecting valuable information. This photograph shows a well-armed (including antitank weapons) scouting party in a *VW-Schwimmwagen*. (Kristofertisch, Oct. 1944)

1./SS-Panzerjäger-Abteilung 1 "LSSAH", November 1944

1. Kompanie

Stab

1. Batterie

2. Batterie

3. Batterie

1./SS-Pz.Rgt. 1 "LSSAH", November 1944

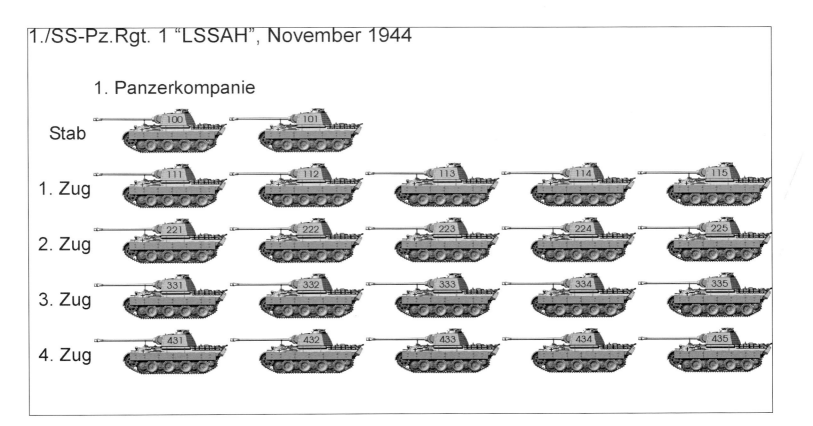

BUDAPEST
OPERATION KONRAD
1 - 26 January 1945

On Christmas 1944, the 3rd Ukrainian Front closed its grip around Budapest, trapping a garrison of five German and four Hungarian divisions. Of the *SS* units, the *18. SS-Freiwilligen-Panzer-Grenadier-Division "Horst-Wessel"*, and the *8. SS-Kavallerie-Division "Florian Geyer"* and *22. SS-Freiwilligen-Kavallerie-Division "Maria Theresia"* were trapped in the city. In this photograph, a *Hummel* from an *SS* unit fires from encircled Budapest.

Hitler ordered the *IV. SS-Panzer-Korps* ("*Totenkopf*" and "*Wiking*") to move from Poland to Hungary, where the two divisions were to spearhead the attack to relieve Budapest. They were transported by rail to Raab (Györ), thereby commencing "*Operation Konrad*". This photograph shows a concentration of armor near Komar on the Danube River. At the time, "*Wiking*" had only 22 *Panthers* and 10 *PzKpfw IV's*. (Grönert, Dec. 1944)

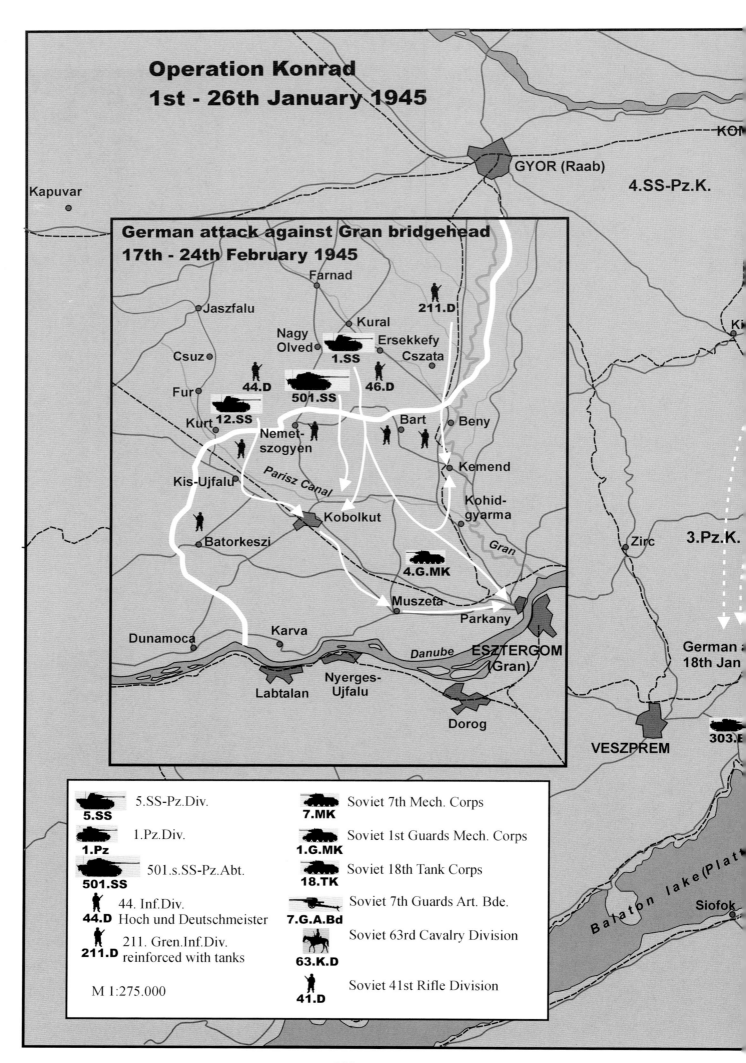

Operation Konrad
1st - 26th January 1945

German attack against Gran bridgehead
17th - 24th February 1945

KOM

GYOR (Raab)

4.SS-Pz.K.

Kapuvar

Farnad

Jaszfalu

211.D

Kural

Nagy
Olved

Ersekkefy

Csuz

Cszata

1.SS

44.D

46.D

Fur

501.SS

Kurt

12.SS

Nemet-
szogyen

Bart

Beny

Kis-Ujfalu

Parisz Canal

Kemend

Kohid-
gyarma

Kobolkut

Zirc

3.Pz.K.

Batorkeszi

Gran

4.G.MK

Ki

Dunamoca

Karva

Muszefa

Parkany

German a
18th Jan

Danube

ESZTERGOM
(Gran)

Labtalan

Nyerges-
Ujfalu

Dorog

VESZPREM

303.

M 1:275.000

	5.SS-Pz.Div.		Soviet 7th Mech. Corps
5.SS		**7.MK**	
1.Pz	1.Pz.Div.	**1.G.MK**	Soviet 1st Guards Mech. Corps
501.SS	501.s.SS-Pz.Abt.	**18.TK**	Soviet 18th Tank Corps
44.D	44. Inf.Div. Hoch und Deutschmeister	**7.G.A.Bd**	Soviet 7th Guards Art. Bde.
211.D	211. Gren.Inf.Div. reinforced with tanks	**63.K.D**	Soviet 63rd Cavalry Division
		41.D	Soviet 41st Rifle Division

Balaton lake (Plat

Siofok

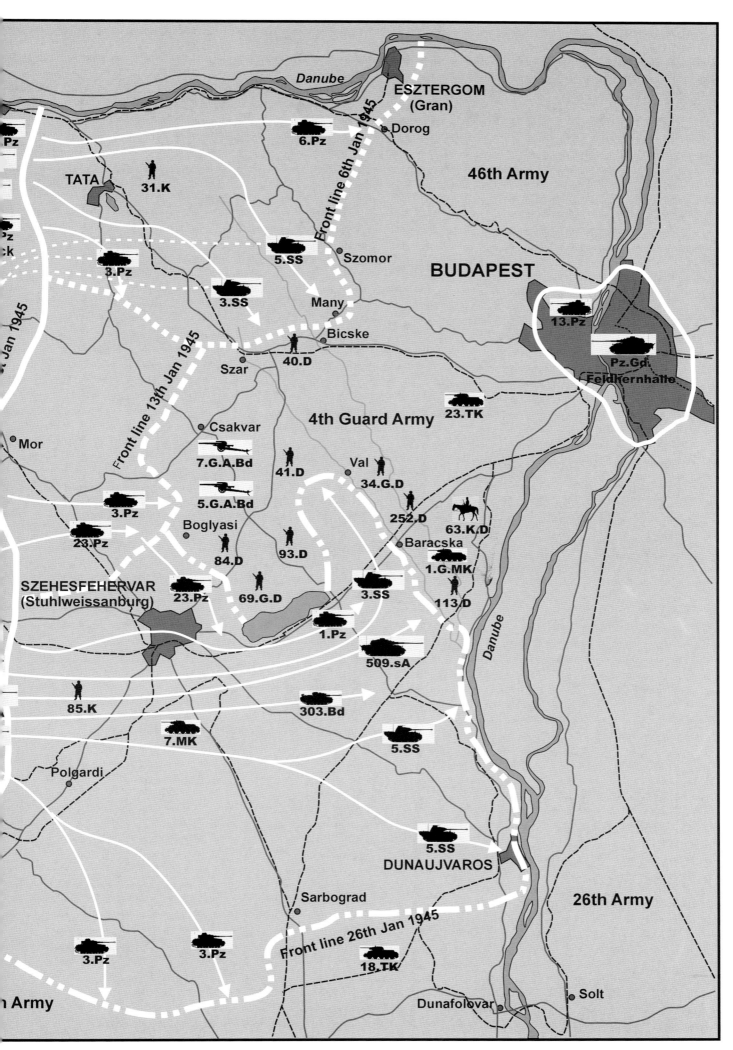

Danube

ESZTERGOM
(Gran)

Dorog

Pz

Pz
ck

6.Pz

46th Army

TATA

31.K

Front line 6th Jan 1945

Szomor

BUDAPEST

5.SS

3.Pz

3.SS

Many

13.Pz

Bicske

Szar

40.D

Front line 13th Jan 1945

**Pz.Gd.
Feldhernhalle**

Mor

Csakvar

4th Guard Army

23.TK

7.G.A.Bd

Val

41.D

34.G.D

5.G.A.Bd

3.Pz

Boglyasi

252.D

63.K.D

23.Pz

84.D

93.D

Baracska

1.G.MK

23.Pz

69.G.D

3.SS

113.D

Danube

1.Pz

SZEHESFEHERVAR
(Stuhlweissanburg)

509.sA

85.K

303.Bd

7.MK

5.SS

Polgardi

5.SS

DUNAUJVAROS

26th Army

Sarbograd

Front line 26th Jan 1945

3.Pz

3.Pz

18.TK

n Army

Solt

Dunafolovar

The commander of *"Totenkopf"*, *SS-Brigadeführer* and *Generalmajor der Waffen-SS* Helmut Becker, studies a map. (Grönert, Jan. 1945)

SS elements advance toward Hungary. In the foreground are an old *Krupp Protze* truck and a *Marder III Ausf. M* self-propelled antitank gun. (Grönert, Jan. 1944)

This interesting photograph was taken in Hungary in 1945 during armored train crew exercises. The German formations on the Eastern Front depended heavily on rail transport and the protection of railways was an important mission. Approximately twenty armored trains, like the one shown in the photograph, operated with specially armed railroad infantry battalions. They were armed with *Flakvierling*, field guns in armored turrets and outdated *Panzer 38(t)* tanks.

Two months of relative peace enabled both divisions to fill up with replacements, so that *"Totenkopf"* arrived in Hungary with 18,800 men and *"Wiking"* with 17,400. Together, the two divisions had about 100 tanks. In this photograph, *"Totenkopf" SS-Panzergrenadiere* wait for the *PzKpfw IV* to move out. (Grönert, Jan. 1944)

Judging by the undamaged side skirt plates, the closest *"Totenkopf" PzKpfw IV* is in relatively good shape, unlike the vehicle in front, which does not have a single plate remaining. Note the worn white winter camouflage. The number "611" on the turret is barely recognizable. (Grönert, Jan. 1944)

On New Year's Eve, both divisions hit the Soviet XXXI Rifle Corps in a surprise attack. They forced it back almost 40 kilometers to the east, destroying about 200 enemy tanks in the process. This photograph shows a destroyed Soviet T-34/85. (Grönert, Jan. 1944)

This *PzKpfw IV* has the turret number "701" painted in red and its *Balkenkreuz* is painted only in black. Its crew is loading rounds through the skirt and turret doors. Note the crew's reversible camouflage smocks. Two tank crewmen wear theirs with the white side out, while one wears the camouflage side out. (Grönert, Jan. 1944)

Following the failure of the offensive in the Ardennes, Hitler intended to improve the situation on the Eastern Front with another offensive. To the dismay of his generals, who had intended to preserve their limited resources for the defense of the threatened German borders, on 8 January Hitler ordered *SS-Obergruppenführer und Panzer-Generaloberst der Waffen-SS Josef "Sepp" Dietrich's 6. Panzer-Armee* to move to Hungary on 8 January. With "Operation Spring Awakening", Hitler intended to destroy the Soviet troops on the west bank of the Danube River and then to liberate the Budapest garrison. Shown in the photograph, taken in Normandy, are Dietrich on the left and *SS-Brigadeführer und Generalmajor der Waffen-SS* Fritz Witt on the right. Witt was killed in Normandy commanding the *12. SS-Panzer-Division "Hitlerjugend"*.

This destroyed Soviet T-34/76 had its turret blown off when its ammunition exploded. Even though the new and stronger T-34/85 was in full production, a significant number of Soviet tanks were still the older T-34/76's.

The German advance was significantly slowed by the Russian antitank guns and mines. When the resistance increased, Gille disengaged his two divisions, bypassed the Soviet defense in a wide arc and hit the LXXXV Rifle Corps with a surprise attack in the morning fog. In four days, the Germans pushed the enemy back 32 kilometers and captured a large number of antitank guns. In this photograph, *SS* troops advance through a Hungarian city. The *SdKfz 10* prime mover tows a captured Soviet ZiS 3 gun. (Grönert, Jan. 1944)

The Soviets mobilized the XVIII Tank Corps in a counterattack, and successfully fended off the the *Jagdpanzer IV's* of *SS-Jagdpanzer–Abteilung 3* (17 vehicles strong). The *"Totenkopf"* and *"Wiking"* were each reinforced with 21 *Jagdpanzer IV's* in July and September. The *"Totenkopf"* also had several *Jagdpanzer IV/70's*, which had the same gun as the *Panther*. In this photograph, probably one of the *"Wiking"* division's 13 *Jagdpanzer IV's* passes a captured Soviet antitank gun. (Grönert, Jan. 1944)

By 24 January, the *IV. SS-Panzer-Korps* and the Army's *1. Panzer-Division* had succeeded in breaking through the Soviet defenses and approaching to within 24 kilometres of Budapest. The last Soviet reserve, the XXIII Tank Corps, succeeded in halting the German breakthrough. This was an opportunity for the surrounded Budapest garrison of 70,000 men to break out. However, Hitler rejected that course of action. This photograph shows a destroyed T-34/85.

12./SS-Panzergrenadierregiment 2 "LSSAH", December 1943

III. Bataillon/12.Kompanie

Stab	2100	2101			
1.Zug	2111	2112	2113	2114	2115
1.Zug	2121	2122	2123	2124	2125
1.Zug	2131	2132	2133	2134	2135
1.Zug	2141	2142	2143	2144	2145

The most favored formation of the *6. SS-Panzer-Armee* was the *I. SS-Panzer-Korps "Leibstandarte SS Adolph Hitler"*, composed of the division of the same name and the *12. SS-Panzer-Division "Hitlerjugend"*. The *"LSAAH"* had 41 *Panthers* and 27 *PzKpfw IV's*, while the *"Hitlerjugend"* had 44 *Panthers* and 40 *PzKpfw IV's*. This photograph shows the *"LSSAH"* on the march. In the column behind the APC, a battery of six *Wespen* is visible and, among them, an obsolete *PzKpfw III* converted into an artillery observation vehicle (Jarolim, Jan. 1945)

The "*LSAAH*" column passes in front of a destroyed Soviet antitank gun. The gun was set up in a very good position, from which it could cover the road. The two visible black lines across the photograph appear to be crop marks made by grease pencil and were drawn by a German war reporter, who was preparing it for publication. (Jarolim, Jan. 1945)

The *"LSSAH"* was reinforced with the independent *schwere SS–Panzer–Abteilung 501*, armed with 36 *PzKpfw VI Tiger Ausf.B* tanks. It was simply called the *"King Tiger"* or *Tiger II*, and had an impressive weight of 70 tons and a frontal armor of 180 mm. Its long 88mm gun could destroy all enemy tanks. However, due to mechanical unreliability, it frequently had breakdowns. Visible in this photograph are vehicles "113", "300" and "321". (Adendorf, Feb. 1945)

This interesting photograph, taken in March 1945 in Hungary, shows a *Panther* from an unidentified unit. The turret bears the three digit number "113", in which the first digit is twice as large as the last two.

The *12. SS-Panzer-Division "Hitlerjugend"* was reinforced with the added firepower of *Panzerjäger-Abteilung 560*, which had 31 *Jagdpanzer IV/70's* and *16 Jagdpanther* heavy tank destroyers. This was in addition to the 20 brand-new *Jagdpanzer IV's* already in the division. The *Jagdpanther* was based on the *Panther* chassis and had an 88mm main gun. In this photograph, a *Jagdpanzer IV* and infantry armed with *Panzerfauste* advance toward the front.

The second unit in the *6. SS–Panzer–Armee* was the *II. SS–Panzer–Korps*, composed of the *"Das Reich"* and *"Hohenstaufen"* divisions. The first had 34 *Panthers* and 14 *PzKpfw IV's*, while the second had 31 *Panthers* and 26 *PzKpfw IV's*. In this photograph, vehicles from the *II. SS–Panzer–Korps* move along a muddy road. Recognizable in the column are two heavy *SdKfz 234/1* armored cars, armed with 20mm automatic cannons. Nineteen such vehicles were included in the armored reconnaissance battalion of an *SS–Panzer–Division*. (Büschel, Feb. 1945)

PzKpfw IV's and APC's are deployed in open terrain. On the left of the photograph is an *SPW SdKfz 250 "Neu"*, a half-tracked APC. It can also be seen in the preceding photograph, and it appears that *SS-Kriegsberichter* Büschel is riding in it. Of interest is the additional armored superstructure. The 1944 tables of organization and equipment for a *Panzer-Division* had 55 such vehicles, assigned to the *Panzer-Aufklärungs* companies. (Büschel, Feb. 1945)

This photograph was taken at the same location. Closest to the camera is an *SdKfz 251/9*, armed with the outmoded short (L/24) 75mm gun, which was redundant after the *PzK-fwIV* was armed with the longer (L/48) gun. This vehicle was designed to provide support for the heavy mechanized infantry company. When zooming in, it is possible to see the turret number "5+01" on a *PzKpfw IV* in the distance, making it a tank of the regimental headquarters. (Büschel, Feb. 1945)

This veteran *SS StuG III Ausf. G* was produced in 1943 and survived to take part in the fighting in Hungary. *Waffen-SS Panzer-Regimenter* used assault guns to augment their weakened *Panzer* companies. *"Das Reich"* had 28, and the *"Hohenstaufen"* had 25 *StuG III's*.

Yet another battered veteran *StuG III*, damaged above the driver's vision block, probably by an artillery shell. It appears that the armor plate is only pushed in, not penetrated. The crew reinforced this weak spot with spare track links and a plate from the skirt armor.

Open terrain and small villages were ideal for armored warfare. Rows of trees along the road are very common in Hungary and are usually the only available cover. Here, *SS-Panzergrenadiere* take their positions along the road. (Jarolim, Jan.1945)

A *StuG* uses a tree as concealment, while the hard surface of the road facilitates a quick change of position. As the hull-mounted gun had a limited traverse of 10 degrees to each side, the driver and gunner had to cooperate closely to turn the vehicle and gun in the desired direction, particularly if there were trees to the front.

SS-Panzergrenadiere use the natural cover of a ditch. Soldiers who took such a position first had a great advantage over their enemy. The soldiers wear the new reversible white/camouflage parkas and trousers. In position, in the background, is a 20mm *Flak*. (Jarolim, Jan. 1945)

A *Flakvierling* mounted on an *SdKfz 7/1* halftrack. This multiple 20mm automatic gun, with a practical rate of fire of 700-800 rpm, had a devastating effect when firing at ground targets in open terrain. In the photograph, the *SS* crew prepares to fire at a ground target. (Jarolim, Jan. 1945)

Judging by the cables and other telephone equipment, these are signals personnel. In case of Russian artillery coming in, entrenchments have been dug a short distance behind them. In the background is a halftrack with an armored cab, which was used as cover when firing the *37mm Flak 36* antiaircraft gun.

The German plans foresaw a small operation, "South Wind", in which the *I. SS–Panzer–Korps* was to destroy the Soviet bridgehead on the western bank of the Gran River. "*Kampfgruppe "LSSAH"*, under the command of *SS–Obersturmbannführer* Jochen Peiper, led the attack. It was composed of the division's tank regiment with *Panthers* and *Panzer IV's*, a battalion of *SS–Panzergrenadiere* in APC's, attached *Tiger IIs* and a battalion of self-propelled artillery with *Hummeln* and *Wespen*. This photograph shows advancing APC's and *Panzer IV's* from *6./SS–Panzer–Regiment 1*. (Büschel, Feb. 1945)

The German attack began during the evening of 16 February. The attack surprised the Russians, and the German infantry succeeded in breaking through enemy lines and pushing forward 8 kilometers, where they encountered a strong antitankgun belt. Peiper sent the *Tiger II*s forward, which destroyed the guns and enabled the infantry to continue the advance. Shown in the photograph are the advancing *Tiger II*s and infantry.

By 24 February, the Russians had been pushed from the bridgehead with losses of about 8,000 men, 71 tanks, 180 guns and much equipment. The *Waffen-SS* lost about 20 tanks and approximately 3,000 men. This photograph shows a captured T-34/85 and, behind it, a *Hummel*.

The *Tiger II's*, which led the main attack and were supported by the *Panthers*, played the deciding role in taking the bridgehead. The Germans used the so-called *Panzerkeil* tactics, in which the tanks were positioned in a wedge formation. In front of *Tiger II* (turret number "300") is a signpost, which reads that it is 45 kilometers to Budapest. (Grönert, Feb. 1945)

The impressive size of the *Tiger II* is best illustrated by the height of the crew on top of the tank's engine deck. Its *8.8cm KwK 43L/71* gun could easily penetrate armor up to 200mm from a distance of one kilometer, enough to destroy even the heaviest Soviet tank. It could destroy a T-34 from a distance of more than 3 kilometers.

PzKpfw IV's and entrenched infantry occupy positions in the Gran bridgehead. Since the tanks are lined up, it appears that this group is preparing to attack. Due to the lack of vegetation for camouflage, the first tanks are covered with dried corn stalks. The closest tank has the number "825" on its turret. (Büschel, Feb. 1945)

This photograph was taken at the same location. It appears that the trench the infantry are in was excavated with machinery. *Sd.Kfz. 251* APC's are visible in the background. (Büschel, Feb. 1945)

It is difficult to recognize *PzKpfw IV* "611" under all the foliage. Its role was to cover the vehicle and to make it difficult to identify.

An interesting photograph of a captured Soviet Su-100 self-propelled gun, armed with a powerful 100mm gun, with the number "466". The gun was dug into the ground and turned into a bunker. (Büschel, Feb. 1945)

Yet another captured Soviet self-propelled gun (SU-85) armed with an 85mm gun like the ones on the T-34/85 tanks. It was very likely damaged and set up as a bunker by the side of the road. Note the *"Totenkopf"* insignia painted above the driver's hatch, through which we can see a crewmember. In the background, a damaged *RSO* halftrack truck and a captured American Jeep are visible. (Weiss, Mar. 1945)

A captured heavy Soviet 152 mm gun position. The horizontal position of the gun barrel shows that it was most probably firing at tanks. In the background is a brand new *StuG III*. (Cantzler, Mar. 1945)

Another view of the heavy gun clearly shows how dangerous it could be. The empty casings show that the crew succeeded in firing off several rounds. A gun dug into the ground like this one was very hard to spot from a tank and, usually, by the time it was spotted, it was too late. The Soviets produced an AP shell for their 152mm gun in 1943 which was able to penetrate 125mm of armor at a distance of 1000 meters. (Cantzler, Mar. 1945)

Surrounded by his officers, an *SS-Hauptsturmführer* from the *"Wiking"* studies a map. His field-grey assault-gun jacket indicates that he is an assault-gun or tank-destroyer unit commander Three of the officers wear the *Panzer* officer's field cap, which was very popular due to its smart appearance and ease of wear. It could be worn comfortably with headphones. The two caps on the far left are converted Army caps with *SS* insignia.

This is an excellent photograph of two *Panzergrenadiere* on the Gran River. Both wear reversible parkas with different camouflage patterns. One carries, over his shoulder, an *MP44* assault rifle with a magazine that used the shortened 7.92mm rounds. The *MP44* became the model for many similar weapons after World War II. (Büschel, Feb. 1945)

A group of *"Totenkopf"* soldiers interrogate a captured Soviet soldier. It is evident that the *SS-Panzergrenadiere* were dressed differently in the winter of 1944/45 than one year earlier. Note that the soldiers are wearing very wide reversible trousers, insulated with woollen padding. (Grönert, Feb. 1944)

SS–Panzergrenadiere and an older version (*Ausf.C*) of the *SdKfz 251*, which was produced before September 1943. Note the large padded mittens on the hands of the standing grenadier, who is about to receive an egg-shaped grenade from a fellow soldier. (Zschäckel, Feb. 1945)

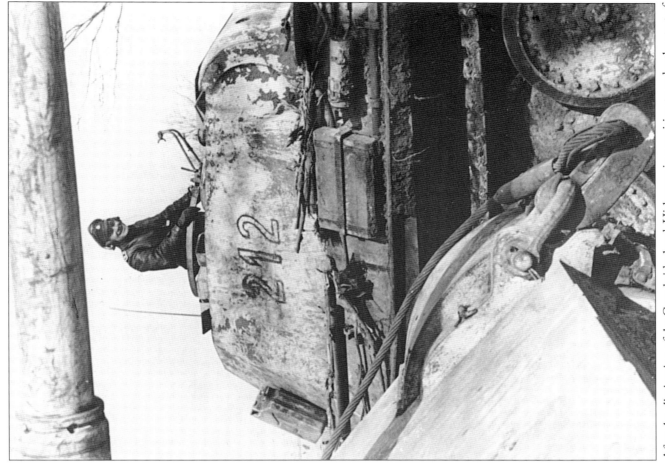

After the elimination of the Gran bridgehead, Hitler was in a position to order the start of "Operation Spring Awakening". The 6th of March was set as the date of attack. By then, an impressive force of 400 tanks had been brought together. This photograph shows the latest *Panther Ausf. G* with a modified gun mantlet. The mantlet's lower part was made thicker and more vertical. Consequently, rounds were prevented from being deflected down through the hull roof. (Büschel, Mar. 1945)

An *SS-Panzergrenadier* in Hungary. Judging by the ammunition belt around his neck, he could be the loader in the machine-gun crew. Note the field cap that covers his neck and ears. It would seem that this is a deliberate pose for the photographer as it was rare for soldiers to fix bayonets.

Five Army armored divisions participated with the Waffen-SS in "Operation Spring Awakening": 1.Panzer-Division (10 Panthers, 10 PzKpfw IV's), 3. Panzer-Division (25 Panthers, 7 Jgd.Pz. IV/70's), 6. Panzer-Division (45 Panthers, 5 PzKpfw IV's) and 23.Panzer-Division (32 Panthers, 5 PzKpfw IV's, 8 Jgd.Pz.IV's). This photograph shows an Army Panther Ausf. G.

In December and January, *schwere Panzer–Abteilung 509* was equipped with 45 new *Tiger II*s and 8 *Flakpanzer*. In mid-January, it was sent to Hungary, where it was attached to the *"Totenkopf"*. This photograph shows the command *Tiger II* of *s.Pz.Abt.* 509 with a large Roman numeral "I" on the turret. (Grönert, Feb. 1945)

The *Panzer IV/70* with the long *PaK42 L/70* gun was an improved version of the *Jagdpanzer IV*, which had the shorter *PaK 39 L/48*. The *Jagdpanzer IV/70* was first used in numbers during the Ardennes offensive. Judging by the partially visible hull number "01" (it could be "001", "101" or "201") and the two antennas, this is a *"Hohenstaufen" Jagdpanzer IV/70* command vehicle. On 6 March, *"Hohenstaufen"* had 24 *Panthers*, 19 *PzKpfw IV's*, 10 *Jagdpanthers*, 16 *StuG's*, and 17 older and newer versions of the *Jagdpanzer IV*. (Weiss, Mar. 1945)

"Operation Spring Awakening" began at 0430 hours on 6 March, with strong artillery fire from the *6. SS-Panzer-Armee*. The photograph shows a position of the 105mm light field howitzers (*10.5cm le FH 18M*).(Weiss, Mar. 1945)

This column of *SdKfz 251 Auf. D's* is probably from the *"Hohenstaufen"*. On 15 March, the division had 141 functional APC's, 41 in short-term repair and 38 in long-term repair. (Weiss, Mar. 1945)

After the combat experience gained the previous winter, the *SS* armored divisions were reinforced with rocket batteries of *Nebelwerfer*. In Hungary, the units of the *6. SS-Panzer-Armee* had several batteries of the *Panzerwerfer*, like these in the photograph. The conspicuous smoke trails from the rockets made it imperative for the battery to change position frequently. The armored *Maultier* semi-tracked truck provides the necessary mobility. The ten-barrelled *150 mm Nebelwerfer 42* was designed for use on the *Maultier*.

The attack began well but, after 15 kilometers, it was slowed down by the numerous antitank guns arranged into Pak-fronts, mine fields and antitank obstacles, as seen in this photograph. Numerous canals were transformed into defensive lines, and they were the greatest hindrance to the armored advance. (Cantzler, Mar. 1945)

This is an interesting photograph of a *StuG III* carrying logs, which could be used to build improvised bridges across canals and small water barriers. Painted on the *StuG* is an interesting black German cross. In the foreground is an *SS Panzergrenadier* carrying a large metal box on his back. This box could contain radio equipment. (Legenberger, Mar. 1945)

A PzKpfw IV moves past dead members of the Soviet antitank gun crew. The ZiS-3 was set up at a curve in the road, which was a typical tactical move. (Weiss, Mar. 1945)

In the open terrain of Hungary, digging into the ground was a priority, and the entrenching tool was an important piece of equipment, carried by the squad leader in this photograph. In the background are what appear to be an *SdKfz 251/21 (MG 151/20)* and *251/22 (7.5cm Pak 40)*, supporting the positions of the *SS-Panzergrenadiere*. (Stille, Mar. 1945)

The operation reached its climax on 12 March along the Sio Canal, where a small bridgehead was established. Due to Soviet pressure, it had to be abandoned. Here we see *SS-Panzergrenadiere* and a *StuG III*. (Cantzler, Mar. 1945)

These *SS-Panzergrenadiere* have been forced to the ground by enemy fire. In the background is the final production model of the *StuG III*. Visible on the vehicle is the *Rundumfeuer MG* (rotating machine-gun), which was operated from a protected position inside the vehicle. (Cantzler, Mar. 1945)

In the period between 6 and 20 March, the *Waffen-SS* divisions suffered substantial losses. Most were below 50 percent of the strength with which they began the operation. The German forces lost 237 tanks and assault guns, 26 field guns and 506 antitank guns in Hungary. By 20 March, the *6. SS-Panzer-Armee* had fewer than 100 operational tanks and assault guns. A powerful Soviet counterattack followed, with no less than 600 tanks and several thousand other vehicles. In this photograph, an *SdKfz 9* prime mover tows an inoperable *StuG III*. (Fade, Mar. 1945)

The retreat of the German forces into Austria, with the end following shortly thereafter. Antitank guns slowed the Soviet advance as much as possible. This photograph shows a *7.5cm Pak 40* in ambush. (Jäckisch, Mar. 1945)

ADDITIONAL PHOTOGRAPHS

This photograph illustrates an interesting approach to defense against ambushes by Russian partisans. The forest on both sides of an important road has been cleared for several hundred meters, denying shelter to lurking partisans. A column of *PzKpfw IV's* and supply vehicles is moving along the road.

In the preserved memoirs of tank crews, there are accounts that the *Panther* was known to carry up to 30 soldiers. This photograph proves that such a claim is not false. The tanks show an interesting variation of colors called the "Ambush" pattern, which was used until the autumn of 1944. It consisted of alternating yellow, green and red-brown spots applied on top of the usual yellow, green and red-brown camouflage. The "Ambush" pattern was meant to simulate light and shadows normally generated by foliage.

If the German tank crews were the elite of the land army, then their mechanics were the elite among mechanics. During periods of intensive armored fighting, they worked on the vehicles day and night, in the toughest weather conditions. This photograph shows a group of mechanics working on the engine and transmission of a *PzKpfw IV*. Note the twin exhaust fans of the engine cooling system.

An *88mm Flak 37* is being towed by an *SdKfz 7* halftrack. Each *Panzer* and *Panzer-Grenadier Division* had several batteries of this dual-purpose gun in its *Flak* battalion. Each battery had from four to six such guns.

An *SdKfz 165 15cm schwere Panzerhaubitze auf Geschützewagen III/IV(Sf) "Hummel"*. The chassis was a hybrid *PzKpfw III/IV* design with a *Panzer III* drive sprocket. The toal number of these vehicles produced was 714. Normally each *SS-Panzer-Division* had one battery with 6 *Hummeln*.

The Czech *Panzer 38(t)* was obsolete as a battle tank by 1942. Reliable and easy to maintain, the TNH chassis was too valuable to lose. During the remainder of the war, its production continued as a self-propelled gun carriage. This photograph shows a *Panzerjäger 38(t) Ausf.M* with a *7.5cm PaK40/3* antitank gun with the complete carriage (minus wheels) installed on top of the superstructure. A total of 975 were produced. The crew was protected against small arms fire from the front and sides by armor plate. This vehicle saw combat service in the tank-destroyer battalions of the armored and infantry divisions.

Newly arrived vehicles in an *SS* unit are being reviewed in 1944. Obviously, a creative artist was responsible for the uniform camouflage pattern seen on all the vehicles; painted green tree branches on top of the yellow base.

A total of 8,500 *PzKpfw IV's*, the workhorse of the *Panzertruppe*, were produced. This photograph shows the most numerous version, the *Ausf. H*, of which 3,774 were built between April 1943 and July 1944. The *PzKpfw IV* was a worthy opponent for the tanks of the Western Allies. However, the appearance of new Soviet tanks, starting in 1944, reduced its role in the fighting on the Eastern Front.

A *PzKpfw IV* is being mounted by a group of well-armed *SS-Panzergrenadiere*. The added *Schürzen* on the sides of the tank were welcomed by the infantry, as their risk of falling under the tracks during transport was reduced.

The firm of *NSU* produced the *Kettenkrad*, a half-ton prime mover designated as a "tracked motorcycle" that was used by all branches of the *Waffen-SS* and *Wehrmacht*. The *Kettenkrad* was ideally suited to covering muddy and otherwise difficult terrain, and was often used by field commanders for short distance cross-country trips. Full-scale production began in 1942, and 8,345 had been built by the end of the war.

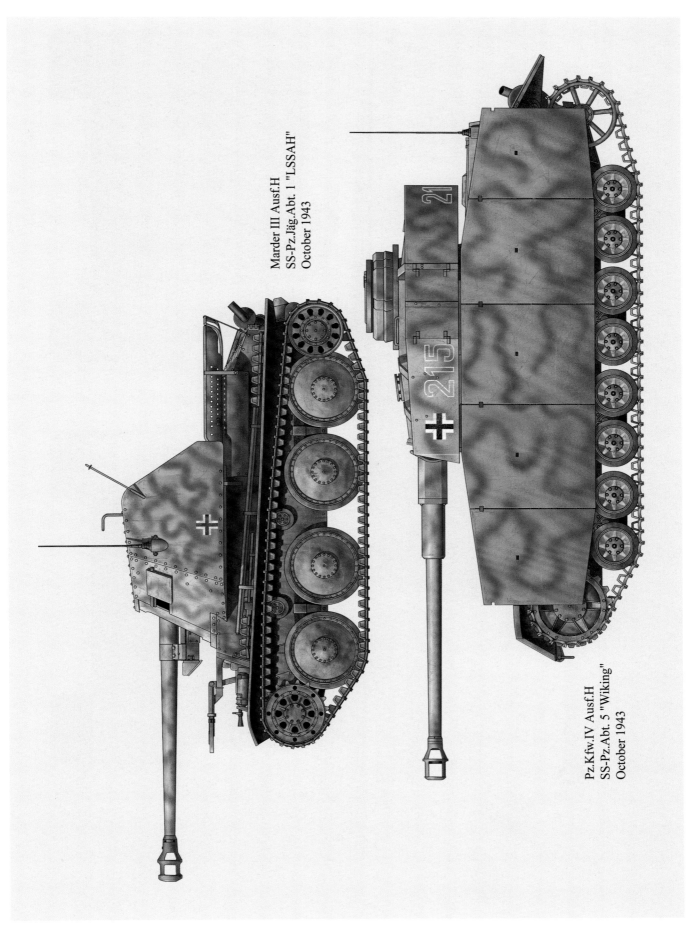

Marder III Ausf.H
SS-Pz.Jäg.Abt. 1 "LSSAH"
October 1943

Pz.Kfw.IV Ausf.H
SS-Pz.Abt. 5 "Wiking"
October 1943

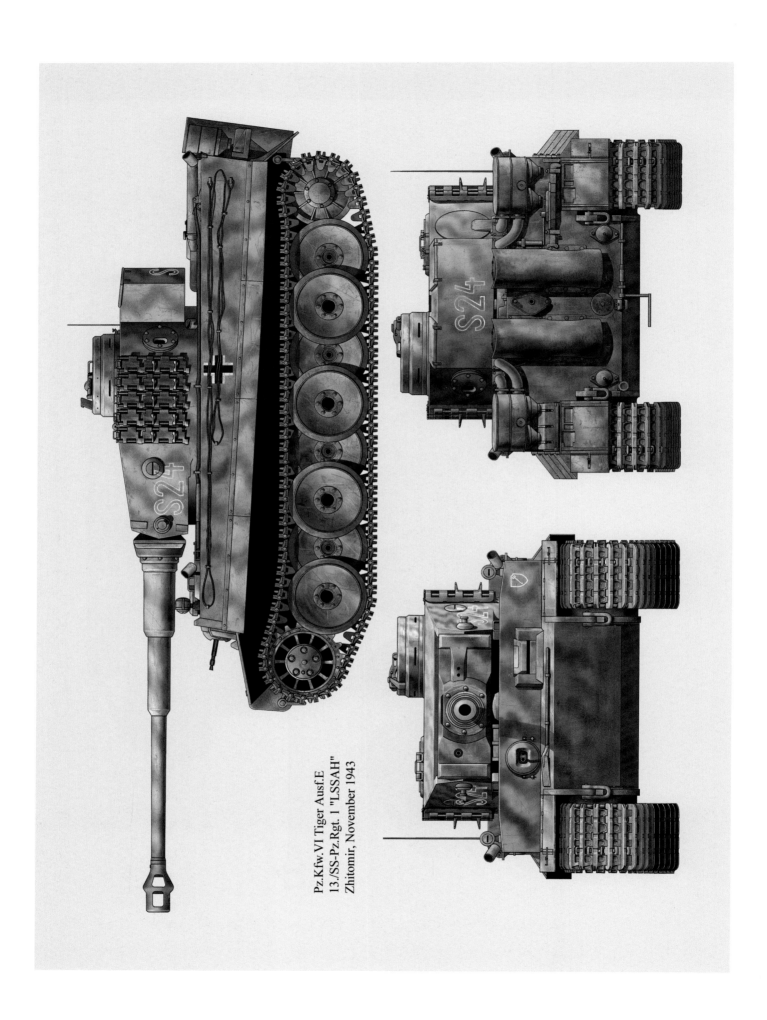

Pz.Kfw.VI Tiger Ausf.E
13./SS-Pz.Rgt. 1 "LSSAH"
Zhitomir, November 1943

266

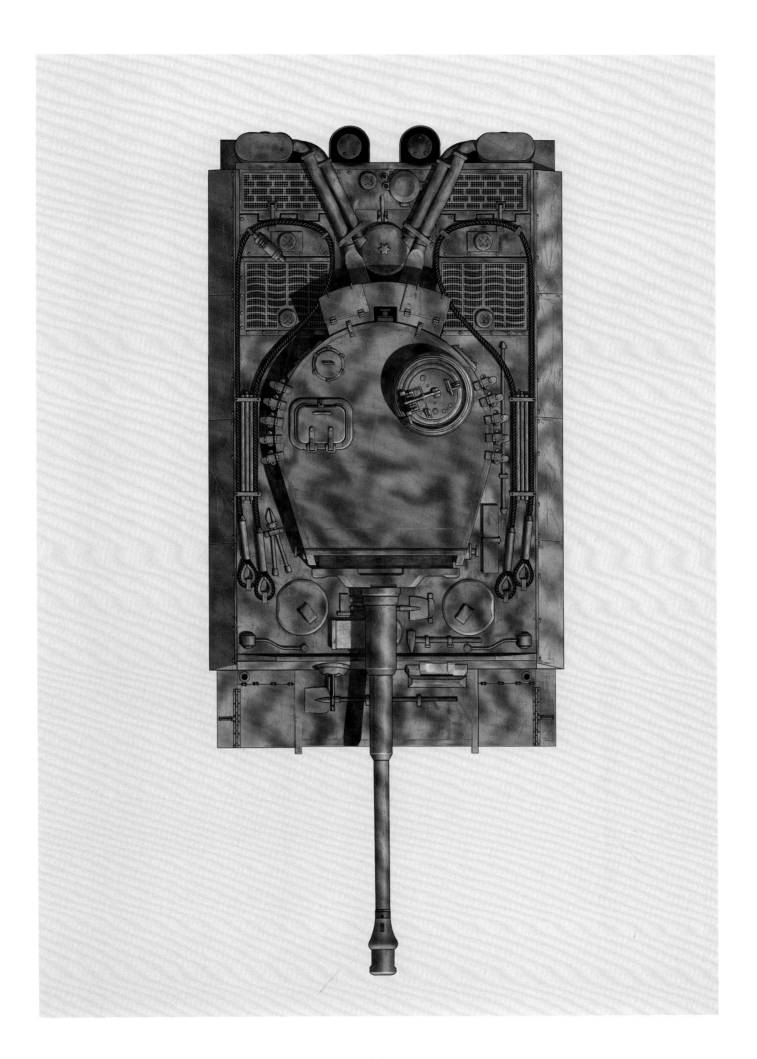

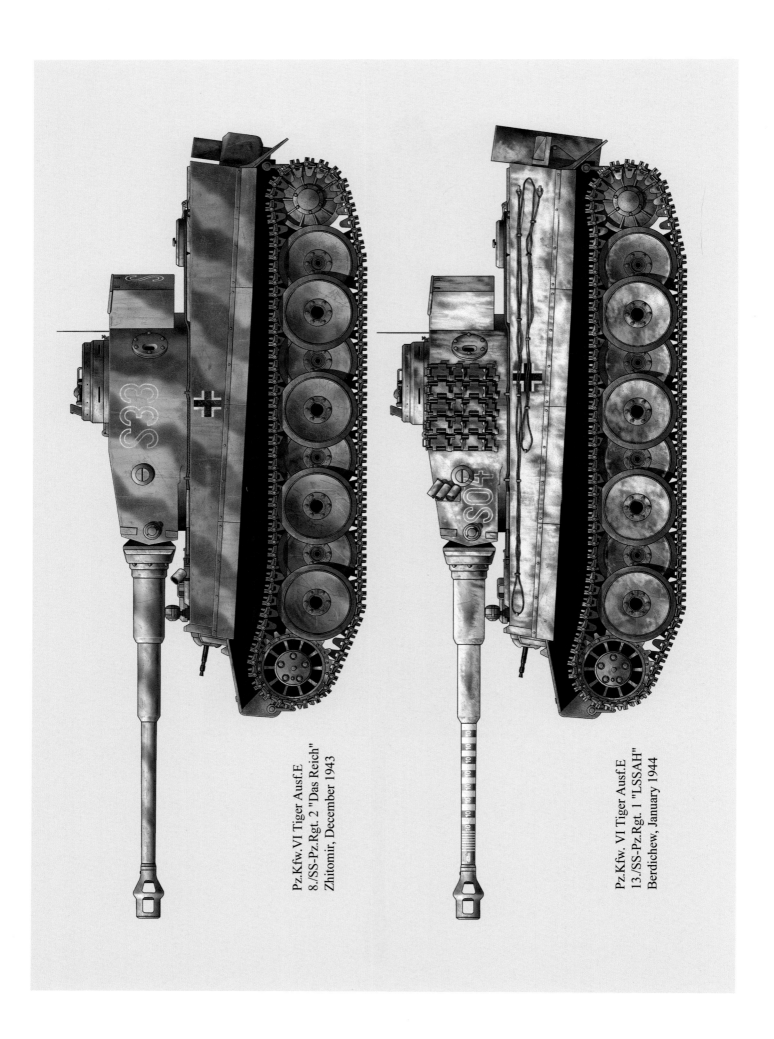

Pz.Kfw.VI Tiger Ausf.E
8./SS-Pz.Rgt. 2 "Das Reich"
Zhitomir, December 1943

Pz.Kfw. VI Tiger Ausf.E
13./SS-Pz.Rgt. 1 "LSSAH"
Berdichew, January 1944

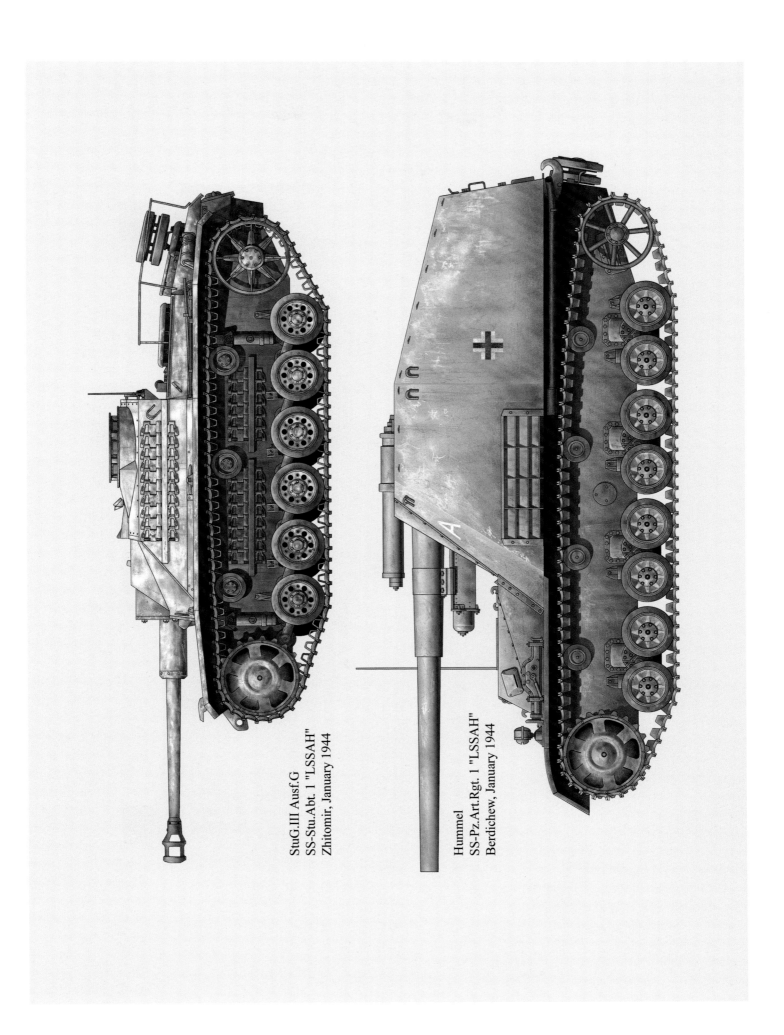

StuG.III Ausf.G
SS-Stu.Abt. 1 "LSSAH"
Zhitomir, January 1944

Hummel
SS-Pz.Art.Rgt. 1 "LSSAH"
Berdichew, January 1944

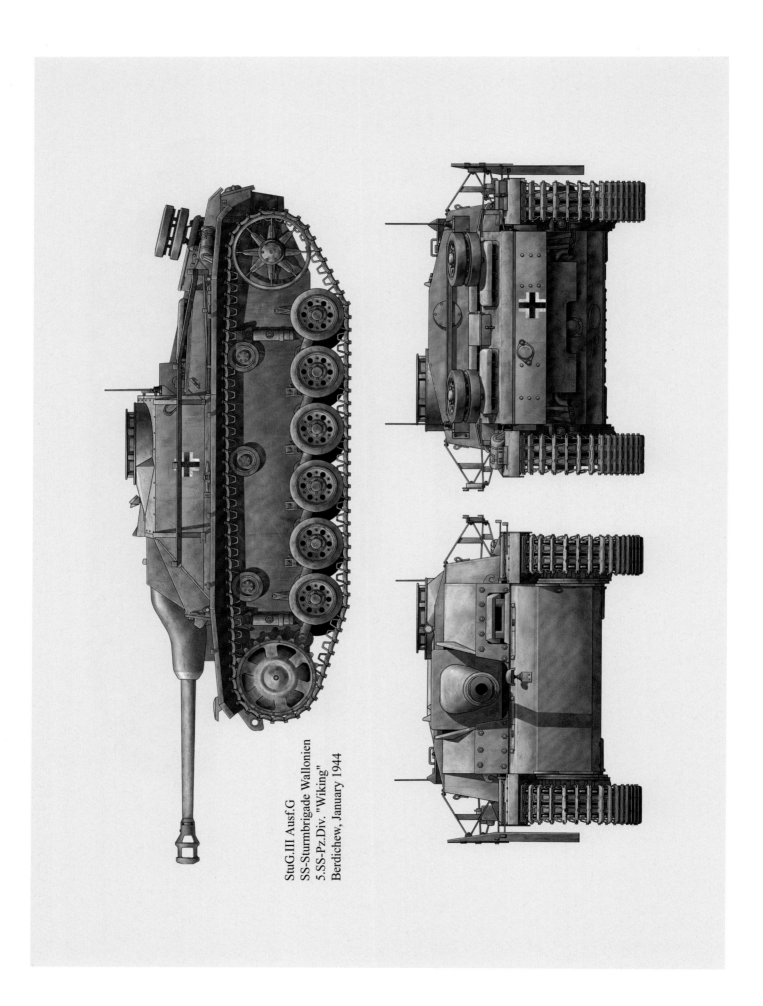

StuG.III Ausf.G
SS-Sturmbrigade Wallonien
5.SS-Pz.Div. "Wiking"
Berdichew, January 1944

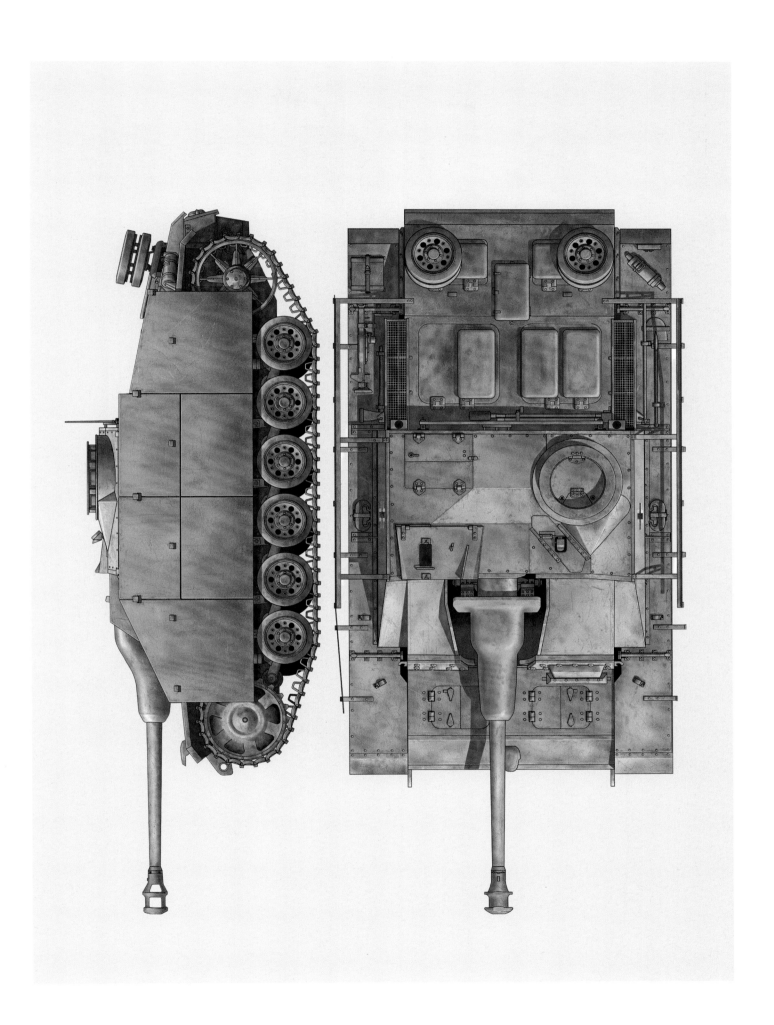

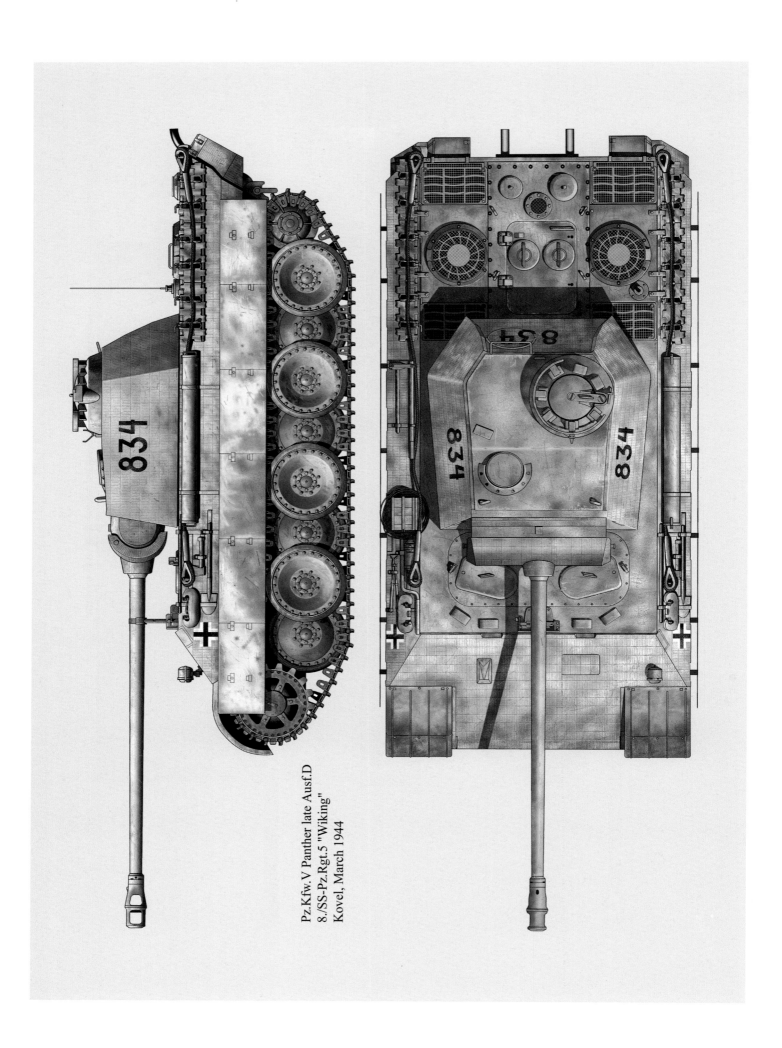

Pz.Kfw.V Panther late Ausf.D
8./SS-Pz.Rgt.5 "Wiking"
Kovel, March 1944

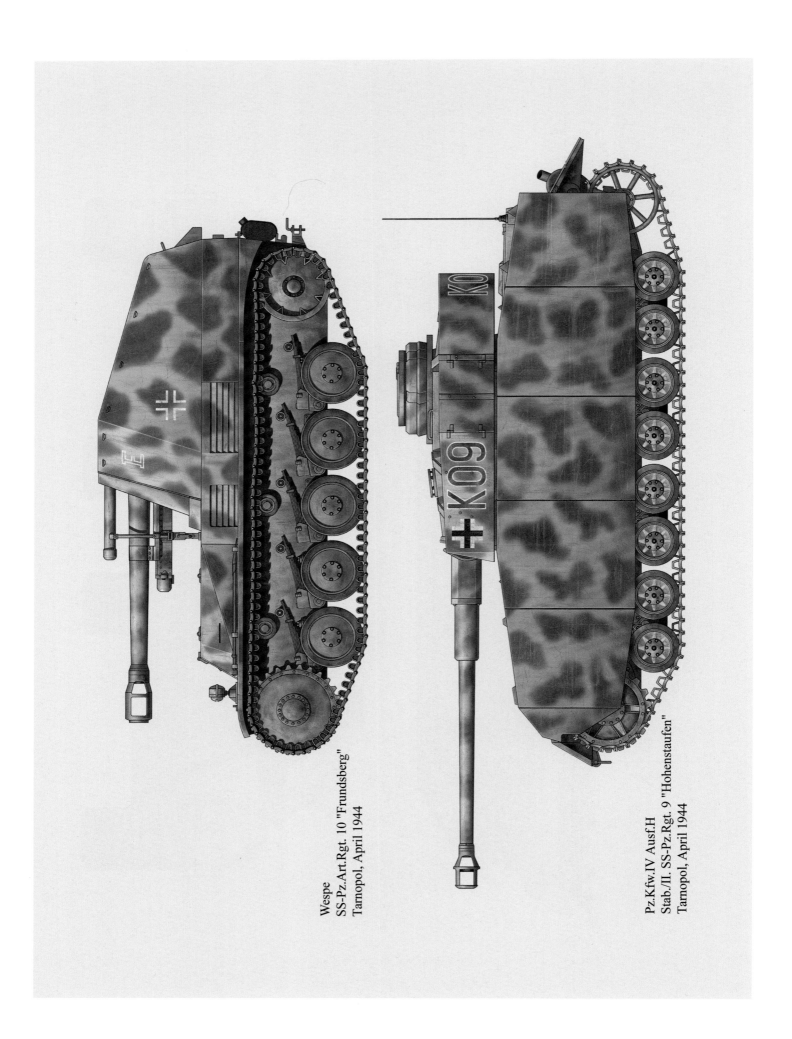

Wespe
SS-Pz.Art.Rgt. 10 "Frundsberg"
Tarnopol, April 1944

Pz.Kfw.IV Ausf.H
Stab./II. SS-Pz.Rgt. 9 "Hohenstaufen"
Tarnopol, April 1944

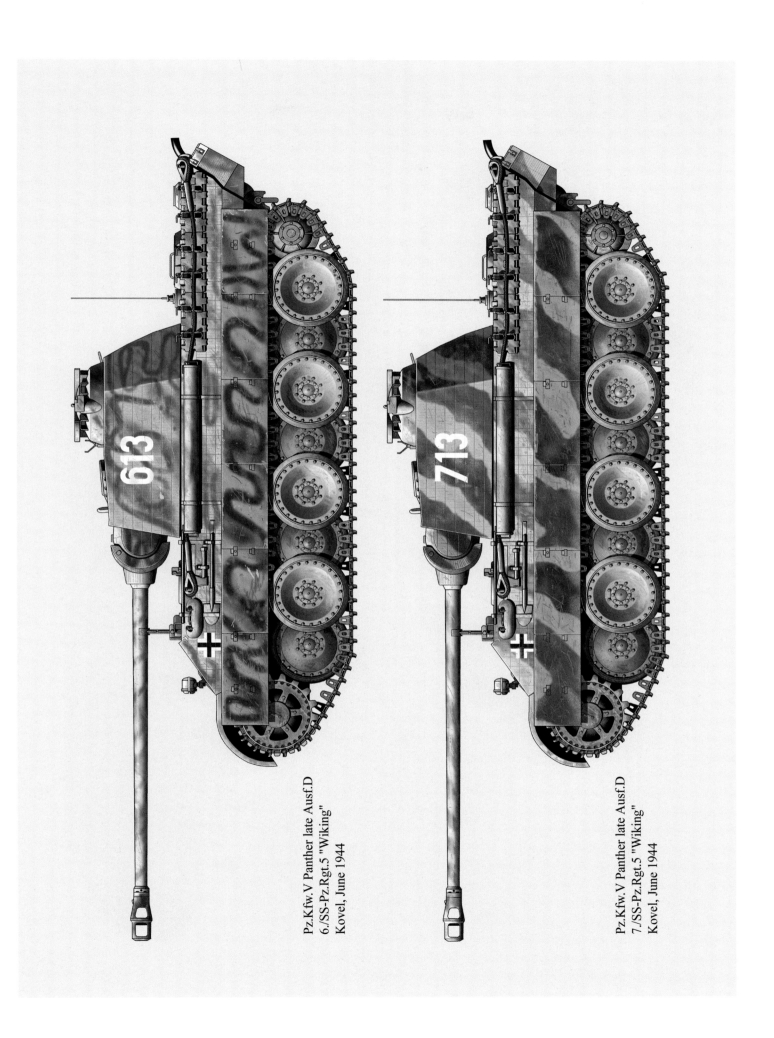

Pz.Kfw.V Panther late Ausf.D
6./SS-Pz.Rgt.5 "Wiking"
Kovel, June 1944

Pz.Kfw.V Panther late Ausf.D
7./SS-Pz.Rgt.5 "Wiking"
Kovel, June 1944

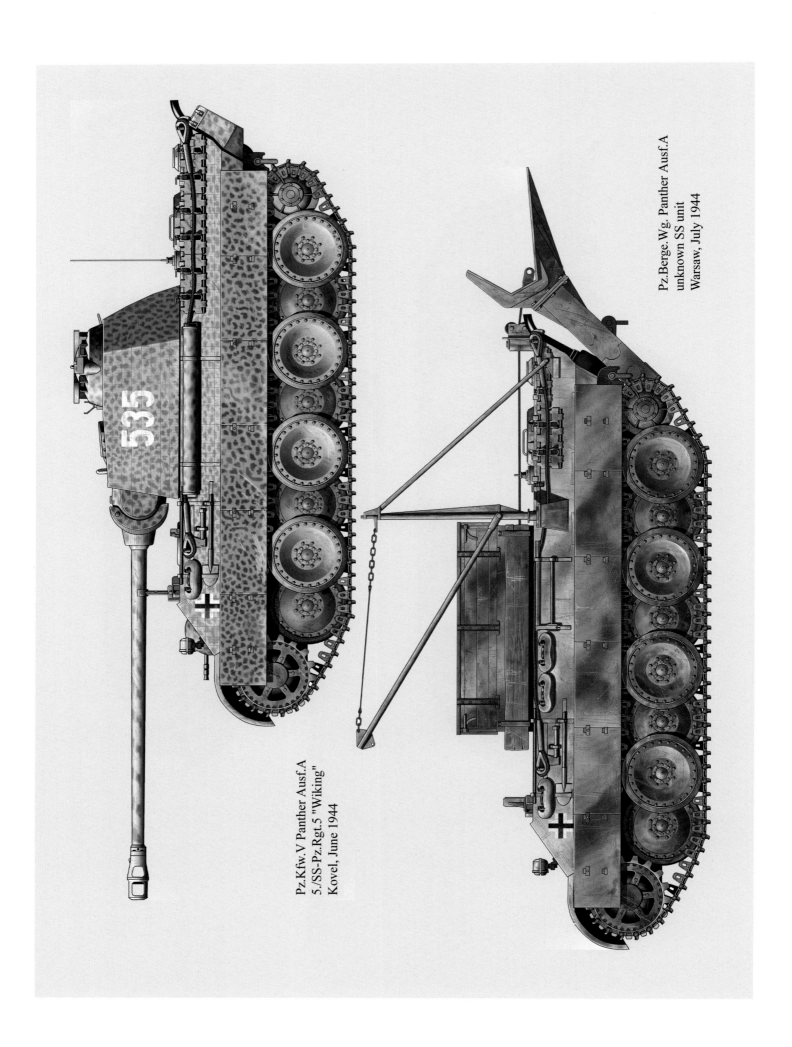

Pz.Kfw.V Panther Ausf.A
5./SS-Pz.Rgt.5 "Wiking"
Kovel, June 1944

Pz.Berge.Wg. Panther Ausf.A
unknown SS unit
Warsaw, July 1944

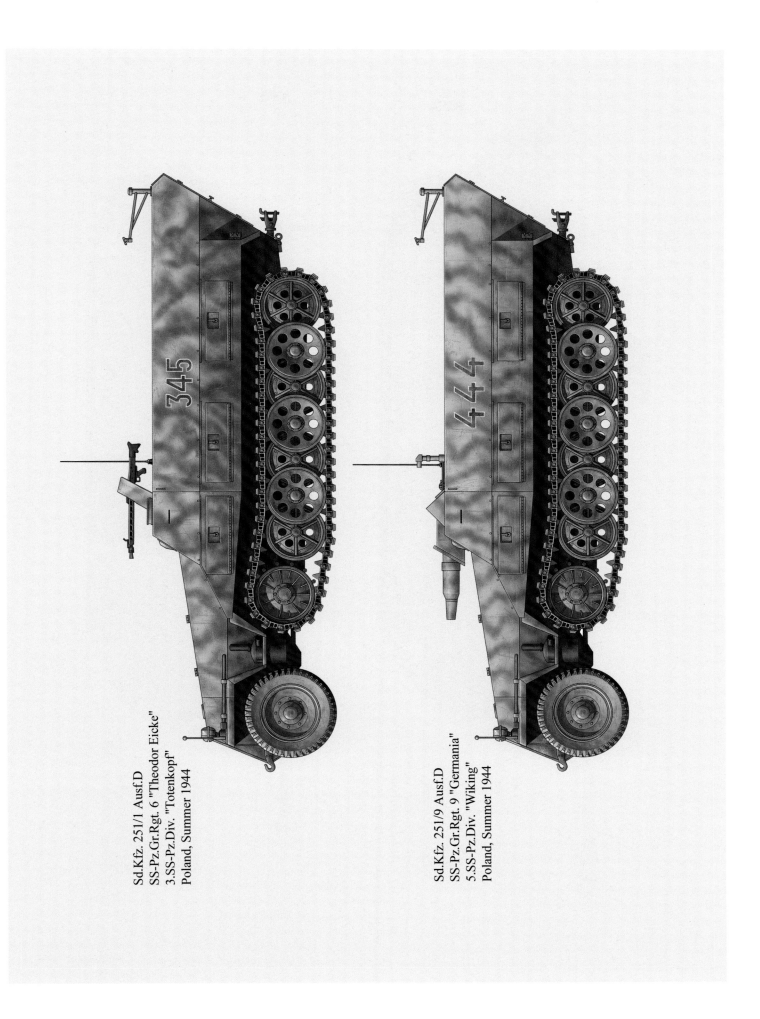

Sd.Kfz. 251/1 Ausf.D
SS-Pz.Gr.Rgt. 6 "Theodor Eicke"
3.SS-Pz.Div. "Totenkopf"
Poland, Summer 1944

Sd.Kfz. 251/9 Ausf.D
SS-Pz.Gr.Rgt. 9 "Germania"
5.SS-Pz.Div. "Wiking"
Poland, Summer 1944

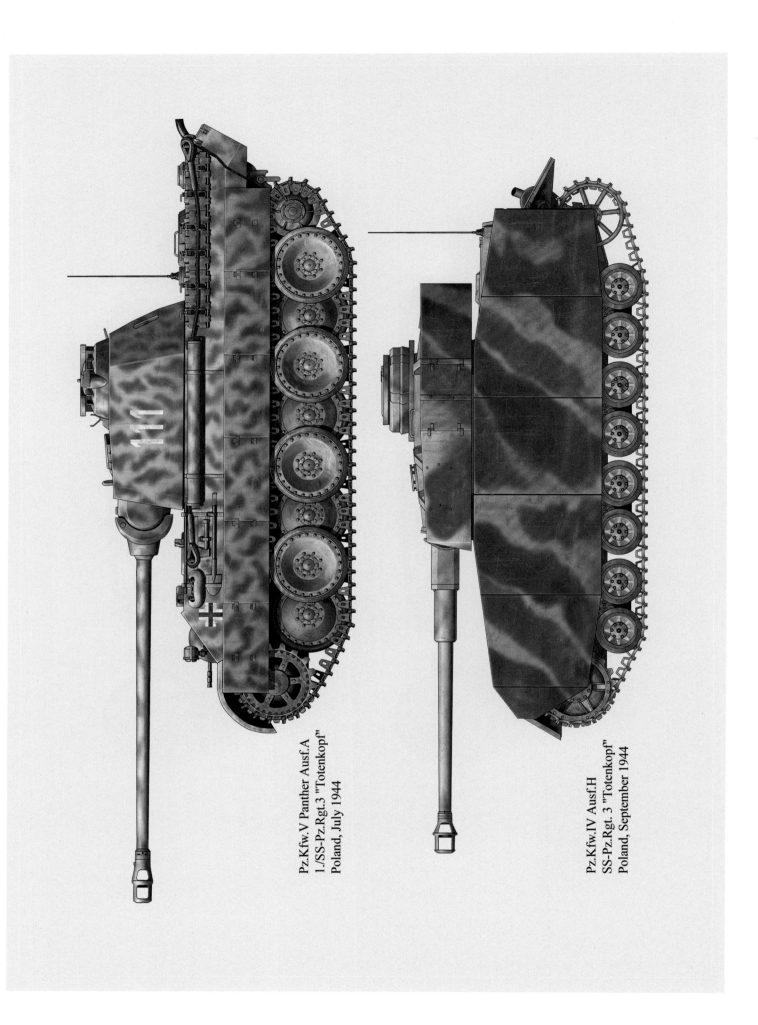

Pz.Kfw.V Panther Ausf.A
1./SS-Pz.Rgt.3 "Totenkopf"
Poland, July 1944

Pz.Kfw.IV Ausf.H
SS-Pz.Rgt. 3 "Totenkopf"
Poland, September 1944

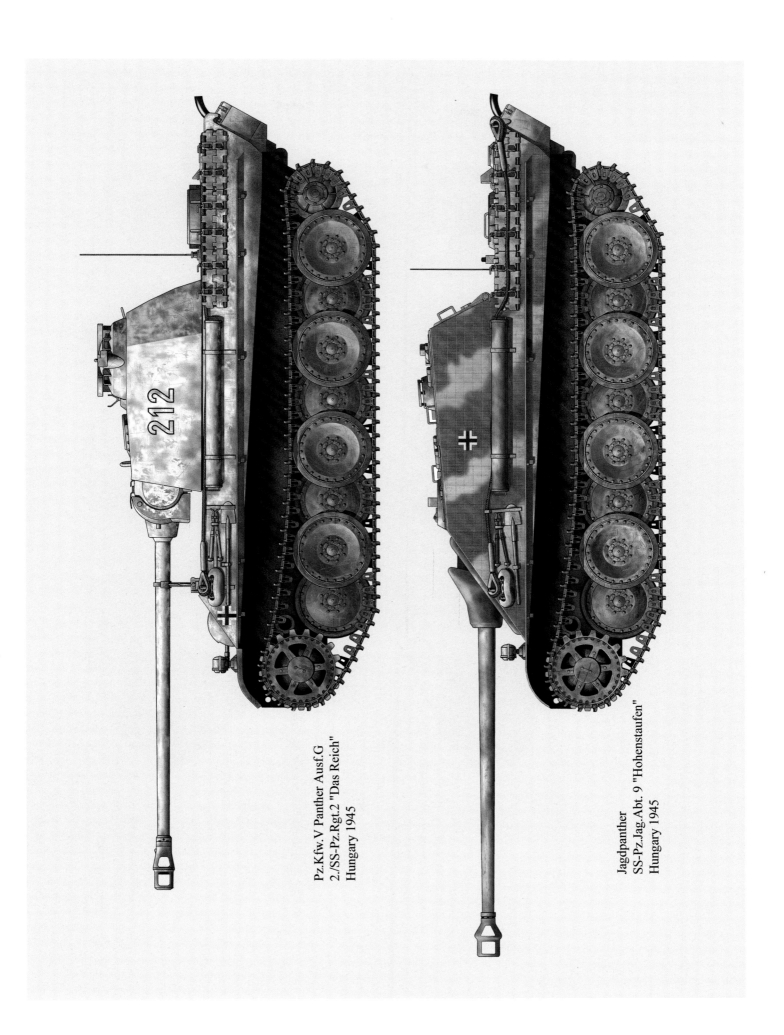

Pz.Kfw.V Panther Ausf.G
2./SS-Pz.Rgt.2 "Das Reich"
Hungary 1945

Jagdpanther
SS-Pz.Jag.Abt. 9 "Hohenstaufen"
Hungary 1945

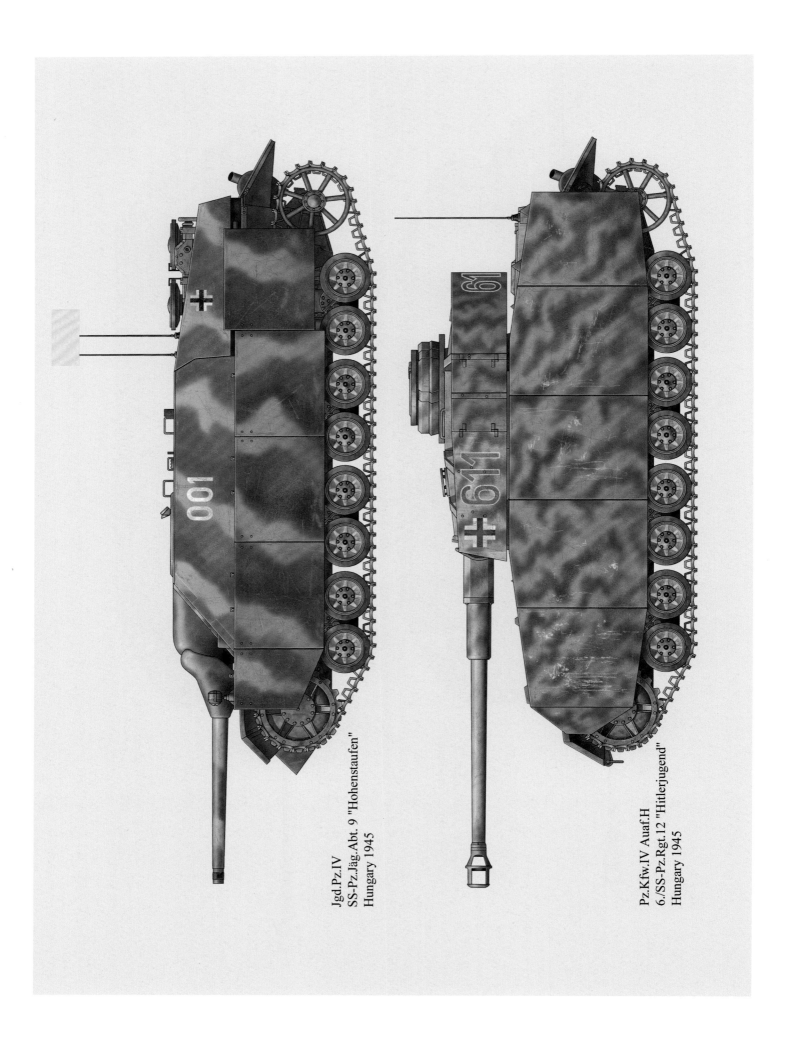

Jgd.Pz.IV
SS-Pz.Jäg.Abt. 9 "Hohenstaufen"
Hungary 1945

Pz.Kfw.IV Auaf.H
6./SS-Pz.Rgt.12 "Hitlerjugend"
Hungary 1945

StuG III's in Hungary, probably from one of the *Panzergrenadier* divisions. The man standing next to the vehicle illustrates well the 2.16 meter height of the *StuG III*. The vehicle's low silhouette gave it a substantial advantage in the open terrain of the Ukraine and Hungary. (Keimling, Nov. 1944)

The lethal *"Acht-Acht"* gun fires from its position. White victory rings, 6 for shot-down aircraft and 12 for destroyed enemy tanks, are visible on the gun barrel. In the summer of 1944, the German forces had 10,930 such 88mm dual-purpose guns.

A welcome meal break for a group of *Waffen SS* soldiers. Note the 1944 pea-pattern camouflage trousers and the popularity of the excellent M 1943 field cap. This cap was so comfortable and popular that it was often worn in combat situations, in strict contravention of regulations! The arm shield on the soldier at the right appears to be that of the *Wallonien* Legion.

A column of *Panthers* moves along an elevated Ukrainian road during the spring of 1944. With the rising temperatures, tanks moving off the rural roads risked sinking into the soft ground and, without the help of another tank or a specialized recovery vehicle, often could not be pulled out of the "muck".

Along with the numerous armored and motorized forces, both sides used cavalry units on the endless tracts of the Eastern Front, particularly in difficult weather conditions. During the winter of 1943-44, small separate cavalry elements were occasionally added to armored divisions, where they were used to scout out enemy positions and for patrolling. This photograph shows an *SS* cavalry patrol in a Ukrainian village.

This series of four photographs was taken in Thessalonica, Greece in the spring of 1944 during a parade of completely new *StuG IV's* of the *4. SS-Polizei-Panzer-Grenadier-Division*. When the threat of Allied invasion in the Balkans became serious, the Germans sent in their divisions to demonstrate their power and to bolster the support of their loyal forces in Greece.

Following the parade in Greece, the *StuG's* of the *4. SS-Polizei-Panzer-Grenadier-Division* were transported to Slovakia to raise the morale of the pro-German regime. In early 1945, the division was engaged in heavy defensive fighting around Stettin and Danzig.

In addition to the seven *SS-Panzer-Divisionen*, seven *SS-Panzer-Grenadier-Divisionen* were also established. They were the *4. SS-Polizei-Panzer-Grenadier-Division*, the *11. SS-Freiwilligen-Panzer-Grenadier-Division "Nordland"*, the *16. SS-Panzer-Grenadier-Division "Reichsführer-SS"*, the *17. SS-Panzer-Grenadier-Division "Götz von Berlichingen"*, the *18. SS-Freiwilligen-Panzer-Grenadier-Division "Horst Wessel"*, the *23. SS-Freiwilligen-Panzer-Division "Nederland"* and the *28. SS-Freiwilligen-Grenadier-Division "Wallonien"*. As their armor component the mechanized-infantry divisions only had a battalion of tanks or assault guns. They fought alongside the armored divisions.

After the Battle of Kursk in 1943, the role of the *Panzertruppe* changed dramatically. Attacks by large tank formations were mostly replaced by defensive actions and counterattacks. The main battle tank lost out in favor of the *Panzerjäger*, *Jagdpanzer* and *Sturmgeschütz*, which can clearly be seen from the production statistics. This photograph shows a *Sturmgeschütz III* from the *4. SS-Polizei-Panzer-Grenadier-Division.*

A column of *Tigers* in the summer of 1944 awaits the command to move out. Longer road marches called for frequent maintenance halts to check for potential running-gear or other mechanical problems. These selected locations had to have tree cover, for increased protection from enemy air attack.

This *Tiger's* track and several road wheels have been damaged by a mine. When even one inner road wheel or torsion bar was damaged, it was necessary to remove 10-14 wheels in order to gain access to the damaged part and repair it. This type of operation was labor-intensive, particularly in winter conditions. This photograph illustrates the type of work required, even though it shows an Army crew at work.

A *Tiger* crew waits for a tow or repairs to its vehicle. The crew has already prepared the vehicle for towing.

The crews of two veteran *PzKpfw IV's* and a *Panther* await the command to advance. Note how the *PzKpfw IV* crews reinforced the front plates of their tanks with spare track links. The *PzKpfw IV's* frontal armor (60-80 mm thick) offered less protection from the new 85 mm Soviet guns that appeared in late 1943.

A group of infantrymen uses a *Tiger* as a shield. Although such protection was useful against small-arms fire, the tanks attracted artillery fire and one round could be fatal to such a grouping of infantry.

A group of *PzKpfw IV's* (one or two companies) prepares to attack, indicated by the positioning of the gun barrels, presumably pointing toward the enemy. Among the tanks, we see a tracked *RSO*, which supplied the vehicles with fuel and ammunition.

All *Panzer* formations received orders to transport tanks by rail whenever possible, even over distances of only several dozen kilometers, to eliminate vehicle breakdowns and to reduce fuel consumption. A company of *Panthers* required a ton of fuel to move 10 kilometers.

The Army crew of a brand-new *StuG III Ausf. G,* camouflages its vehicle with debris from the surrounding ruins. Note the *Zimmerit* anti-magnetic paste, which was rarely applied to the entire vehicle. The pattern that featured small waffled squares was used on vehicles produced by the MIAG factory. The crewman on the left wears the badge for the single-handed destruction of an enemy armored vehicle, an award not frequently seen on an armored vehicle crewman's uniform.

PzKpfw IV tanks, like this one from the *"Hitlerjugend"*, easily knocked down large trees. However, tank commanders avoided such actions, which could easily damage the *Schürzen* and throw track. Initially, the skirts were hung vertically on hooks from the side rails and were easily damaged by even small terrain obstacles. On later models, as seen in the photograph, the side skirts were positioned at an angle, lower on the hull and closer to the wheels, to reduce potential damage.

Rank Comparison Table

US Army	German Army	Waffen-SS	Commonwealth Forces
Enlisted			
Private	*Schütze*	*SS–Schütze[1]*	Private
Private First Class	*Oberschütze*	*SS–Oberschütze[2]*	(None)
Corporal	*Gefreiter*	*SS–Sturmmann*	Lance Corporal
Senior Corporal	*Obergefreiter*	*SS–Rottenführer*	Corporal
Staff Corporal	*Stabsgefreiter*	*SS–Stabsrottenführer[3]*	(None)
Noncommissioned Officers			
Sergeant	*Unteroffizier*	*SS–Unterscharführer*	Sergeant
(None)	*Unterfeldwebel*	*SS–Scharführer*	(None)
Staff Sergeant	*Feldwebel*	*SS–Oberscharführer*	Color Sergeant
Sergeant First Class	*Oberfeldwebel*	*SS–Hauptscharführer*	(None)
Master Sergeant	*Hauptfeldwebel*	*SS–Sturmscharführer*	Sergeant Major
Sergeant Major	*Stabsfeldwebel*	(None)	Regimental. Sergeant Major (RSM)
Officers			
Second Lieutenant	*Leutnant*	*SS–Untersturmführer*	2nd Lieutenant
First Lieutenant	*Oberleutnant*	*SS–Obersturmführer*	Lieutenant
Captain	*Hauptmann*	*SS–Hauptsturmführer*	Captain
Major	*Major*	*SS–Sturmbannführer*	Major
Lieutenant Colonel	*Oberstleutnant*	*SS–Obersturmbannführer*	Lt. Colonel
Colonel	*Oberst*	*SS–Standartenführer*	Colonel
(None)	(None)	*SS–Oberführer*	(None)
Brigadier General	*Generalmajor*	*SS–Brigadeführer*	Brigadier
Major General	*Generalleutnant*	*SS–Gruppenführer*	Major General
Lieutenant General	*General der Panzertruppen etc.*	*SS–Obergruppenführer*	Lieutenant General
General	*Generaloberst*	*SS–Oberstgruppenführer*	General
General of the Army	*Feldmarschall*	*Reichsführer–SS*	Field Marshal

(Footnotes)

[1] *SS–Mann* used as the rank designation prior to 1942.

[2] Rank not used prior to 1942.

[3] This rank did not exist officially, but it has been seen in written records.